Sinéad Brady is Founder and lead career and work psychologist at A Career to Love. She lives in Cavan, Ireland and works globally as a speaker and consultant to organisations. Sinéad advocates for a workplace that is fair, equitable and human-centred, one where everyone has the opportunity to thrive, flourish, and progress. *Total Reset* is her first book.

TOTAL RESET

TOTAL RESET

Quit Living to Work and Start Working to Live

SINÉAD BRADY

HarperCollins*Ireland*

HarperCollins*Ireland*
Macken House
39/40 Mayor Street Upper
Dublin 1
D01 C9W8
Ireland

A division of
HarperCollins*Publishers*
1 London Bridge Street
London SE1 9GF
UK

www.harpercollins.co.uk

First published by HarperCollins*Ireland* 2023

1 3 5 7 9 10 8 6 4 2

A catalogue record for this book is available from the British Library

ISBN: 978-0-00-855296-1

Set in Meridien LT Std by Palimpsest Book Production Limited,
Falkirk, Stirlingshire

Printed and bound in the UK using 100% Renewable
Electricity by CPI Group (UK) Ltd

To Alan, Saíbhe, Saórla, Siún, and Senán.

This book is for you, written with the deep desire that it sparks a conversation that improves the world of work and how we choose our careers for you and the generations that follow.

CONTENTS

PREFACE

This book is about an idea. It is an idea with roots in the 1950s, but which holds incredible, almost unbelievable, sway over how we make decisions today – decisions about our lives, our work and our careers. This defining idea of our times is that our work and our careers are *the* most important, all-encompassing aspect of our lives and should take precedence over all else. This idea is directly connected to our current 'always on' culture, and stands at the core of the relationships we have with our work, our careers and our identities. During the 1950s, and the decades that followed, work and our careers began to occupy a more central position in our personal lives. This happened as the result of a perfect storm between technological advances in how we worked, the movement of our places of work to large urban centres, and the shift from working for survival to working for meaning. This trio of complex intersecting parts has arguably led to the almost religious worship of our careers over and above all else, including family and friends, even when it makes us sick.

What is work?

On the surface that question appears basic, but once you dig a little deeper its complexities are revealed. Over the past fifty years we have experienced a slow but collective shift in our psyche around the function of work in our lives. Work was once a simple transaction: you traded a finite amount of your time, expertise and qualifications in exchange for a salary. That salary provided financial security for you and your loved ones. In that world, once you did your job and the workday finished, you went home. The idea that you went to work to explore your true passions, or to explore how your identity and career connected was an almost entirely alien concept.

Shift forward to 2023, and while work remains central to our financial security, it has also taken on a new and complex meaning for us. Such is the centrality of our work and career to our personal identity that we often wonder 'without work, who am I?'

From the first time that you're asked 'What do you want to be when you grow up?' the seed of an idea is planted, that you should by rights find that *one* thing you are destined to do. What is that *one* career that holds the promise of revealing our authentic real self? As we each pursue the one, our thoughts and actions should be focused. We even know how we should feel when we find the one: time should pass differently, accompanied with a sense of becoming more alive, more centred and more vibrant, both in life and in our career. In time we are expected to understand that this connection between career and identity is something fundamental to our being, and that we should work harder and harder, longer and longer to achieve it.

But what if I told you that this way of thinking is a house of cards? One that is making us sick, and taking its toll on our mental health? You likely won't be surprised – in fact you may feel relief. You may already feel that the emphasis placed on the idea of some deep sense of connection between who you are and what you do has gone too far.

Yes, you want a career that you love to live in but you also want to be able to freely live life while having a career. Yes, your career is important to you, and it is part of your identity, but it is not *all* of who you are and what you are. Failure or a mistake in your career is upsetting, yes, but it does not mean that *you* are a failure or a mistake. The loss of a job or a missed promotion hurts, but when that hurt leads to a cascade of self-doubt and/or depression, or fuels an underlying belief that you are not good enough, you are in trouble.

Before we go any further, I am not for one second suggesting that this is your fault. It is not. The social and cultural narrative of our workplaces and schools, and the public policies upon which they are built, have created 'rules' that underpin these feelings.

Universal 'truths'

The established fallacies around work and careers – that you should find a career that defines you, and that that career should be the most important part of your life – act as self-fulfilling prophecies. The truth is that long-held beliefs (which were originally grounded in evidence and research, but which have since been debunked as falsehoods) remain highly impactful on our decision-making process about how we work, where we work and the careers that we choose.

We live in a world where our careers are so central to our lives and identities, yet the methods we use in choosing our careers are very often carried over from a time very different from our own, and no longer reflect how we live or indeed how we work. In short, the world of work is broken, and it no longer serves us.

The rules of this world were written for a different time and fail to account for the game we are playing. And for that reason we need new stories, new rules and new narratives if each of us is to truly thrive, flourish and progress in life, work and career.

The message at the heart of this book is that you are not just your career, and your career is not all of you. Your career is part of your identity, not the entirety of it. When you go to work your organisation, team, boss or leader does not own you. The skills, abilities and talent that you possess, and your time, either inside or outside of work, belong to you. Work is transactional by its very nature; you exchange a defined amount of your time, alongside your skills, talents, abilities and subject matter knowledge, in return for pay, progression and experience.

The broader social environment of an always on, hustle culture helps us to forget this notion. This can make us feel in some ways that we are owned by our employers in return for pay. To succeed you are expected to work long hours and to 'fit within their culture. In order to 'fit' you'll likely need to undertake resilience, stress and time management training – skills you need in order to do more work in less time.

Yet as you emerge from this training nothing has changed in the organisation to facilitate you in this endeavour. Key performance indicators (KPIs), 100% billable hours, deadline upon deadline and little time to eat, sleep or spend time with people who make you smile are elements of our working lives that have become commonplace for far too many of us. In these environments, it's almost inevitable that we become increasingly stressed, anxious, sad and burned out. The large organisations that report on this epidemic of workplace ill-being consistently publish reports that warn of presentism, lack of engagement, career dissatisfaction and productivity gaps, all contributing to employee burnout.

You know this feeling if you have ever carried yourself towards your two-week annual leave looking forward to the break, only to find yourself sick on holiday. When you work so hard that your annual leave ends up as a time of recovery rather than rest, you are in a dangerous loop.

We need new narratives for a new way of working. New ways of thinking about our careers, our lives and our work. As we emerge from the mass shock that was Covid-19 we find ourselves at an unprecedented moment in the history of work, with unprecedented opportunity for change.

As an individual I hope this book and the information that it presents you with gives you room to breathe as your career follows the ebbs and flows of life. As you read, it is my wish that you realise that you do not need to be more, that having a career and having a life are not mutually exclusive endeavours.

If you are reading this as an organisational leader or a person of influence, my wish is that it provides fresh insight into the impetus and origins behind some of the diversity, equity, inclusion and belonging agendas that you are pursuing. These pursuits are both noble and important, but they need more than plans, policies and procedures to have a real-world effect: they need action.

The world of work is broken, but not irreparable: the only solution is to change the system, and yet for some reason we keep attempting to change the people. By exploring the history behind the phenomena we see all around us in the world of work at the moment – quiet quitting, 'workism', the Great Resignation and the blurring of work–life boundaries – and by looking at the ideas that influence how we think about our jobs and our careers, I hope this book brings you a better understanding of what it means to truly have a career to love, and how it *is* possible to reset your relationship with work and build a sustainable career.

HOW TO USE THIS BOOK

Before we begin

This book is set up in three parts, with each serving a different function. Throughout each, I will focus on breaking open the myths upon which we have made our career choices. Throughout the book, you as the reader will be invited to get involved in the process, which feels only right, for this is your career and you are no idle bystander.

Part One – Perspective

Making new career choices, or indeed any choice, can be stifling. The perspective we hold, our world view, and the accompanying beliefs of that perspective are informed by the spaces and places we find ourselves in. Families, friends, government policies, social norms, cultural expectations – each plays a role in how we make decisions, including decisions about our careers. The focus of the chapters in Part One is to take you on an informative deep dive into the broken world of work, and the myths that our careers are built on. It shifts the focus, and the blame, away from you as an individual who has made 'mistakes' towards a more nuanced, contextual understanding of a broader, fundamentally flawed system.

It outlines how our education system, our policies and our practices are all unwittingly setting us up for failure. It serves to remind us that the way we have chosen careers to date is not only outdated but dysfunctional. It breaks down the myth that there is a single career out there waiting for you and that one day it will suddenly find you.

Part One is called Perspective as it aims to highlight exactly how and why the world of work and the structures it is built upon are broken. With curiosity it shines a light on the myths that our career-making decisions are built on, and how those falsehoods lead to an unsustainable career. As we close Part One, we focus on the hallmarks of an unsustainable career, and how you can identify if you have one. Armed with this perspective, you shift your world view, and from that new space have the ability to see things differently.

Part Two – Reset

In Part Two we begin to reset our relationship with our careers and explore what a sustainable career is. This involves the process of resetting, or stepping outside, the models of thinking used to support career choice before, and choosing a different, more suitable one for you. This does not suggest that you should forget all that has gone before; rather it requires a shift in thinking towards an alternative paradigm, one that places you at the heart of your career rather than the other way around.

The topics in Part Two ask you to jump in and become active in your career. The ideas are novel, emerging from new critical research, but they are also practical and based on my work with many thousands of people and organisations. Hopefully they offer a breath of fresh air in supporting you in your endeavour to find success.

Embarking on a total reset involves the courage to create new alternatives, fit for the future, rather than based on the past. It is from a position of rest that a sustainable career is introduced, alongside the tools you need to create it. To achieve this, you will encounter your momentous moments, career shocks and catalysts; as you take an unfiltered Career Selfie, you begin to collate the data required to design your own success, in the form of a sustainable career.

In Part Two, with courage to illuminate your path, you collate and collect the information needed to create a sustainable career.

Part Three – Success

Finally, in Part Three, together we get very practical. Our focus is on figuring out 'what next' – specifically, what success designed by you, for you, looks like during this season of your life. To achieve this, we will bring together all the information you have collated, explored and learned in Parts One and Two. Using this data, we connect the dots between you in the present and your future.

Much of what you will do in Part Three is self-reflective and action-based, as it orients you towards a sustainable career, one that works for you during this season of life, so that you can thrive and progress in life *and* in your career. I will then take a final look back, at both the core messages of the book, and how those messages guided the very writing of this book at every stage.

How this book will help you

This book is for you if you are ready for change in how you live your life and perform your career. Yes, you are ambitious and eager to succeed, and a meaningful career is important to you, but not at the cost of a meaningful and happy life beyond the remit of your work.

This book can help you if you want to better understand what it means to have a sustainable career while living a meaningful life. It does not offer a magical fix for the out-of-hours phone calls, emails or IMs. Nor does it suggest a way to manage the weekend work, or to get the type of work pattern that you want. It will not match you to the perfect career or perfect job. That is an impossible promise that I could not make in good conscience.

Instead, my promise is threefold.

First, this book promises to break open the myths upon which our current world of work is built, and in so doing deconstruct the incredible sway they hold over our decision-making processes in our work and careers. The purpose of this is to help you to better understand the deeply flawed system within which you have been taught to make career and work-related decisions.

Secondly, I promise to support you as you answer questions about what work means for you in the broader context of your life. Together we will challenge the 'rules' that operate silently in our world of work so that your vision for a sustainable career, one designed by you for you, is realised.

Thirdly, I promise to support you in your journey to design a sustainable career for yourself – and also for those who will follow along the paths we create. You are at the frontier of something new; the path that you choose, along with others who read this book, is paving a new, better future, not just for you but for the generations to come.

The collective energy of challenging the old rules and the

system that we know to be broken will tip the scales in favour of something better. A workplace revolution is what we need. For it is through the collective and diverse voices of many that real meaningful change is realised.

Key concepts

As each reader is unique, you will each choose to engage with this book differently. You may choose to write, or not, to read in sections, chapter by chapter, or until you reach a full stop at the end of a page. You may sit on public transport or in your car as you listen to the audio version of this book. So how you decide to integrate the moments for reflection into the story of your career is entirely up to you. I would, however, suggest that you familiarise yourself with each concept, what it means, and consider how you can engage with it over the course of this book. If you are so inclined, you might also consider moving from thought to action as you test how you can use the ideas or concepts in any aspect of your work, life or career.

Pause for 60

When you come across the phrase 'Pause for 60', this is your invitation to stop reading for 60 seconds, to drop this book and pick up a pen and your notebook to reflect on a specific idea, point or topic that you have just read about. You can use a notebook that makes you smile when you look at it and keep it to exclusively record your career-related thoughts.

Integrated into each Pause for 60 are prompts to help you focus your reflection in a meaningful way. This is an optional addition to reading the text, and if you would prefer not to

Pause for 60, or if you are reading this on public transport, or for whatever reason it isn't convenient, that is not a problem, although you will find there are many benefits from the process.

In those 60 seconds it is suggested that you focus on writing, doodling, mind mapping – really whatever works for you to get the thoughts in your head down on paper.

Why write?

You might wonder, and rightly so, why I would ask you to write. Research shows that when you write you engage a range of senses in your fingers as you touch the pen. As you start to write, draw or doodle, your brain, when examined under fMRI imaging, lights up like the brightest star-filled sky you could imagine. Your brain remains activated across multiple domains long after you have finished writing.

This helps to explain why so many of us find writing or drawing to be a relaxing and therapeutic experience. It also gives us an understanding as to why so many people find that when studying if we write something down, we are more likely to remember it.

As you scan the page and consider what you have written, or drawn, the visual cues provided to your brain, through your eye, provide a complex feedback loop to your brain. This process, along with the feedback loop, primes your brain to engage in creative thinking. This form of learning is hard to replicate under other circumstances.

So, as you journey through this book and learn to reset your relationship with your career, these moments of Pause for 60 will help you to connect, reconnect and construct all the information from your career, past and present, and link it to your future.

Permission Mindset

Typically, when we think about permission it is about getting permission from someone else; when that permission is (or is not) granted, our decision making is accompanied by a sense of entitlement, or lack thereof, to do what you want, or need, for yourself. In the context of this book, a Permission Mindset is about allowing yourself to challenge deeply held beliefs about the world of work and careers.

A Permission Mindset is therefore permission from yourself to yourself to think freely, to be curious, to ask questions and to free yourself of the rules that have previously guided your decision-making process. To critically address narrow conceptualisations of what it means to be ambitious and successful.

When activated, your Permission Mindset will help you to clearly think about the point at which your work, life and career intersect, and as you do that you consider that intersection in the context of the rich tapestry of your life.

Agency and your career choices

Through this book, I am keen to deconstruct the notion that you are 100% responsible for your career, because let's be clear here, there are times when what happens to you in your career are beyond your control.

The notion that you as an individual have complete agency or autonomy to make decisions about your career in isolation from the other parts of your life is a dangerous belief that has many of us working harder and for longer hours not for our own benefit or well-being but to increase the bottom line of a business or organisation. No amount of resilience training, productivity hacks, bananas in the canteen, upskilling or other perks can account for unethical behaviour, overt greediness, or a basic lack of humanity.

With that in mind, we'll look at the story of your career as one chapter within your overall story. That story has a past, present and future that is connected to you, inter-dependent on others and connected to society and to the organisations in which you work. You don't have to share that story with everybody, but what is important is that you understand it for yourself. And once you understand it for yourself, you can reconcile it and better understand how to achieve a sustainable career that will complement your life, not dominate it.

PART ONE

Perspective: The Ability to See Things Differently

CHAPTER 1
The World of Work is Broken

The world of work is broken. The ways in which we choose our careers – a choice that determines our place in the world of work – are fundamentally flawed. Everyone, from the overworked nurse to the stretched teacher, busy admin staff, IT workers, plumbers, painters, electricians, accountants, retail staff and everyone in between, on some level knows this to be true. The framework of how we think about work and our careers is inherently flawed, and for many of us the place where this flaw initially makes itself known is when we are kids, deciding for the first time just what we will spend the rest of our lives doing. In an endeavour to better understand this, let's first look at the state of play – at how our flawed systems are harming us, and at the 'solutions' currently being offered to help solve the problem. Then, let's unpack and deconstruct some of the myths upon which we make choices about our working lives and careers.

When our work affects our health

Each year research undertaken by academic scholars and large global management consultancies confirms our intuition that something is very wrong with how we work, and how we choose our work. In 2022, Gallup, a global workplace consulting and research organisation, published its annual *State of the Global Workplace* report, finding that only 21% of the world's employees are engaged.[1] At the time of writing, according to the American Bureau of Labor Statistics, 65% of the working population in America are actively searching for a new job.[2] In Europe, that figure, according to Eurostat, is 41%.[3]

According to the European Agency for Safety and Health at Work, 44% of Western European workers feel stressed at or about their work, and 46% associated that stress with time pressure or work overload.[4] Other significant contributing factors to that stress included lack of autonomy and control over the pace of work or the processes by which work is carried out. That feeling of stress increased due to poor communication within or co-operation across the organisation. Globally, according to the World Economic Forum (WEF), only 33% of the 27,000 employees it surveyed in 2021 felt as if they were thriving in their work, while in 2022 Gallup found that only 11% of workers in Southeast Asia reported feeling well at work.[5] The same report showed that working women in the US and Canada were the most stressed globally.

The cost to organisations of this disaffection in 2022, according to the WEF, was an estimated $7.8 trillion in lost productivity. It is maybe telling that the estimated cost in dollars at the individual level is not given. It is not as easy to measure a feeling by tracking output, so for the most part we don't even try.

Joint research carried out by the International Labour Organization (ILO) and the World Health Organization (WHO) support these findings. The study, carried out between 2000 and 2016, with findings published in 2021, found that people who worked over 55 hours per week were more likely to die from ischaemic heart disease and stroke.[6] Workers living in the Western Pacific, Southeast Asia, men and older people were identified as those at the greatest risk. The fact that this particular ILO/WHO study did not account for the additional hours of work associated with unpaid domestic labour suggests that if unpaid labour were included the figures would be likely to increase, and would highlight the impact of long work hours on a wider demographic across all genders.

This level of disengagement, and the associated health risks, could and should be considered a global mental health crisis. As I write these words, we continue to be encouraged to work long hours, hustle on the side and remain constantly switched on for our employers.

The workplace wellness industry

To right this wrong, the workplace wellness industry has sprung up, estimated by the WEF to be worth $4.4 trillion globally. Ideas to bolster wellness at work range from on-demand coffee to free training, lunches and lunchtime yoga. Then there is resilience, unconscious bias and productivity training. In recent years some of the training that you are offered is ironically delivered through lunch and learn sessions, the very time when you should be taking a break from work, nourishing your body and relaxing so that you can work productively in the afternoon.

No matter what way you look at it, the world of work, in its current format, fails *everyone*. The ensuing effects, as we struggle to balance having a fulfilling career with living life, impacts *all* people, at *all* levels, in *all* organisations, across *all* career stages.

But how did the best-educated, most advanced generations of people in the history of the world get to this point in our collective experience? The complexity of that question alone is immense, but together let's try to gain deeper insight.

Careers and the age of fulfilment

At this point it is important to give some context to these pretty bleak statistics. Collectively, we are the first generation where the dream is to trade up from money to meaning in our careers, and in doing so, our noble quest is to find a source of existential satisfaction from our work. In short, we are living in and through an age where the desire for fulfilling work and a career that provides a deep sense of meaning and purpose has replaced our need for survival. It is no longer enough to have a career that provides a good salary and job security so that you can put food on the table and pay the mortgage or make rent. We want more.

And there is nothing wrong with that quest, or our desire to find a meaningful career, one to which we feel connected. Suggesting otherwise would be hypocritical of me since my life's work is dedicated to doing just that. Each day, in and through my work, with individuals at all stages of their career journey, and within the organisations that I partner with, I strive daily to help people find a career that they love to live in.

As part of my work within a wider community of work and organisational psychologists, alongside vocational scholars, social, coaching and clinical psychologists, workplace practitioners, and HR thought leaders, who use a critical lens to better understand the world of work and careers, we endeavour to help our generation, and those that follow, to find a space of contentment and happiness in work and in life, not one or the other.

The question we really need to ask ourselves is, how have

our careers – the part of our lives from which we are told we are meant to derive meaning – become one of the greatest sources of discontent in our lives? What is really going on, and how did this happen to us? The answer is WEIRD . . .

WEIRD data

WEIRD is an acronym for Western (men), (well) Educated, (living in) Industrialised, Rich and Democratic (societies). This term was put forward by an American evolutionary biologist named Joseph Henrich to describe the background of the majority of those who participated in psychological research in the social sciences during the 1950s. The fundamental assumptions underpinning research from this era was simple – all humans share fundamental cognitive, behavioural, biological and emotional characteristics. Therefore it was believed that any large enough sample of humans would be capable of revealing fundamental truths that represent the universal experience of *all* humans. Differences in gender, ethnicity, culture, socioeconomic background, education, or wider life experiences were viewed as irrelevant. This is one of the foundational errors that our current world of work is built upon.

Findings based on this WEIRD demographic were presented as representative of the universal experience of *all* humanity, despite representing only 5% of the global population. Such is the persuasiveness and pervasiveness of this logic that it has invaded our understanding of everyday life. WEIRD data would go on to underpin medical research, instruct global education policies, inform research agendas, influence infrastructure design and bolster political campaigns. In numerous ways, this data is still influencing all of these things today.

From the 1950s onwards, the wider world of work began to use this 'neutral evidence' to design, develop and build its structures, processes and cultures, influencing every single aspect of them. The IQ tests, selection and assessment procedures, leadership models, job design portfolios, linear career paths, performance metrics, standardised work patterns and workspaces that we all take for granted evolved from this flawed data. This fundamentally skews the entire framework used to support our understanding of human behaviour and serves to entirely neglect the lived experience of 95% of the population.

And yet, even though the academic world knows this logic is fundamentally flawed, and that this data does not – in fact could not – represent the other 95% of the population, such is the saturation level of this logic that we continue to believe that it is representative of the whole truth, and nothing but the truth.

This is not our fault. A small movement within the social sciences began from around 2005 to raise the question within the academic community of whether research based on 5% of the global population could truly be seen as representative of the lived experience of all of humanity. This movement pointed to the fact that basing our assumptions upon this biased and imbalanced research fundamentally skews our understanding of human behaviour, positioning the 95% majority in the minority.

Yet still, empirical data based on WEIRD people continues to be produced and presented as representative of all. But this new data is based on the findings of the original data, so the starting point is in fact false. What's more, according to *Psychology Today*, 50% of the research published in leading industry gold-standard journals in the developed West and applied globally is carried out by researchers living in three postcodes in the US.[7] This is even the case in published research that depends on variability for legitimacy. For example, a study into this by Cambridge University scholars found that a staggering 96.7% of participants in cross-cultural and evolutionary psychology publications – studies that often depend on diversity for accuracy – are WEIRD, with 81% of the sample from WEIRD demographics.[8]

That means that the research we rely on to make decisions about our careers and work lives is for the most part based on 5% of the world's population, half the time undertaken by researchers living in just three US postcodes. The result of this is that a huge amount of what we *think* we know about the world of work, careers and how they are connected to our lives is premised on conclusions drawn from inadequate and often flawed data.

This does not mean that anyone who falls within the criteria of WEIRD is inherently bad, or intentionally biased, or indeed that the research that used this demographic as its core focus was intentionally wrong. In fact, the efficacy and reliability of the research was excellent at identifying and building a world of work that opened opportunity to and for the demographic it studied. It is worth noting, however, that men from this small, very specific demographic represent 70% of CEOs globally.

The crux of the issue for you and I today is that the application of this decades-old flawed data has influenced the structures, cultures and beliefs that most of us operate within. It has led to structural and cultural inequalities in accessing basic healthcare, education and, most importantly for the subject of this book, our shared ability to work and live.

The birth of the ideal worker

As a result of those early studies from the 1950s, and the resulting body of research that grew out from that early sample, an idea developed – that of the ideal worker. The ideal worker during this era was stereotypically male and married. He was wholly dedicated to work, sternly focused on linear career development, and prioritised work above all else, including family and life outside work. He was expected to be 'always on', available to the organisation day or night, ready to travel, or relocate for work, and to prioritise career success over family or leisure. Sound familiar?

That same social narrative simultaneously spawned another idea, the perfect pairing to the ideal worker – the ideal homemaker. She (for the homemaker was invariably a woman) was defined as a wife and a mother. She, like her husband, was always on, except her focus was expected to be on her role within the family home, where she performed as a domestic goddess, existing to support her family 24/7. She too was expected to be a willing traveller, ready to relocate to support and care for her family, all the while prioritising family over her career success.

For the ideal worker, the world of work was, at least in theory, a relatively straightforward place. Talent, ability and skill played their roles in career progression, but tenure, continuous employment, visibility, length of service and the ability to play office politics were significant and contributing factors to success. Workplaces structured on these norms tended to define a career as both linear and continuous.

For the ideal homemaker, the domestic world was one in which she took pride. A tidy home, with the smell of freshly baked bread and home-cooked food, was central to her success. Her ability to throw a good dinner party and to attend to all of the cooking, cleaning and nutritional needs of her husband and children was also essential.

Books, magazines, TV advertising and education prepared her for this role, and that same social narrative lives on in numerous ways today. On my own wedding day, my grandmother gifted me the book she was given on her wedding day, a book that described in detail how to be a good wife. Dating from this very era, her well-thumbed book explains how to help your husband relax after a long day in the office, which includes changing his shoes and socks while he sits in his relaxing chair. As you do this you offer him his favourite drink. Ideally, talk to him about his day, but only if he is up to it. If you have children, you should keep them quiet during this time, and if you talk about yourself, it's best to only offer up details of your day if asked. As you perform your role as domestic goddess, naturally you are expected to wear nice shoes and inviting clothes. To this day, I am not sure if my grandmother was serious or playing with me. These days, whenever she calls to us for dinner or evening tea, she tells me, every single time, that I am very lucky because my husband is as good as another woman in the house.

So closely intertwined were these archetypes of the ideal worker and homemaker that in the mid-twentieth century, if a young married male executive was seeking a promotion, his employers commonly interviewed his wife. The focus of that interview was partly to confirm she could fulfil her role as homemaker and partly to determine if she would support the longer working hours the promotion would mean for her husband.

As time went by and women entered the paid workforce in greater numbers, they inevitably found themselves attempting to meet the criteria of the ideal worker themselves. Thus, many women found themselves trying to meet the demands of not one but two flawed archetypes. Over the intervening 70 years the model of the ideal worker grew to be a workaholic, intensifying his or her paid working patterns across their lifetime, egged on at every turn by the systems of work they laboured within.

The changing world of work

At the point when these archetypes were being most firmly established, in the middle of the twentieth century, many jobs were secure and permanent until retirement, or death, whichever came first. This was a time before Nokia and BlackBerry allowed our work to follow us wherever we went, when the only way to contact you outside of work was to write a letter, send a fax or call the landline in your home. After clocking out on Friday, or when you went on holidays, nobody contacted you – ever.

Then, the working clock became 24/7: late nights, early mornings and work-based socialising were presented as badges of honour that displayed career commitment. These badges, worn with pride, brought with them the promise of career progression within your current organisation or, if necessary, in a new one.

As the permanent pensionable job slowly disappeared between the 1980s and early 2000s, work became and has continued to become less secure and more precarious. The resulting shift in the employment contract brought with it the necessity to work harder and longer hours to keep your job. As the world of work became faster, more agile and more digitally based thanks to new technologies, slowly it seeped into our non-work lives. Logging on in the evening to clear those last few emails has become more and more expected from employers and in turn by colleagues.

As the pace of life quickens, despite being overwhelmed, always on and harbouring a deepening dissatisfaction with our work–life balance, the ideal worker of the modern era keeps going. Even when suffering from burnout, work-related stress or a lack of engagement, the ideal worker is incited to keep on doing, to keep on being productive because their work performance – they are led to believe – reflects their achievement in life.

The more the boundaries between our careers, our work and our lives blurred, the more our collective sense of dissatisfaction grew. Yet, from the outside looking in, all the boxes were ticked: the ideal worker had a great career that paid well and a nice house in a good location; could afford to buy new cars, go on foreign holidays and buy plenty of clothes.

Don't get me wrong; there is nothing wrong with your work making this type of lifestyle possible. It is only right that in return for your wage you can live, buy food and clothes, put a roof over your head and meet medical bills. The thing is, work and our working identity *are* now so central to our lives that it is impacting our general well-being and our overall sense of self.

Some people have made it to the top of their career ladders, and others have found a career that they love, but most of us are struggling to reconcile our life, career and work with the unrealistic expectations of the ideal worker. We are so busy trying to be the ideal worker that most of us don't have the privilege of time to stop and think about the broader picture of the world of work, that the systems we try to make ourselves fit in are the true cause of our unhappiness with our careers.

In contrast to this we are, inadvertently or directly, told that *we* are the problem. The narrative is recognisable:

'You can have it all, and more, if you try hard enough.'

'Never give up, especially when it's hard – how to become more resilient.'

'Work–life balance and how you can have it.'

The subtext to these headlines is clandestine but clear: if you want to be successful and happy in your career it is entirely up to *you*. What we are not told is that very often the structures and systems pressuring us to achieve unattainable standards are outside our immediate control.

The unseen influences on your career

Having a career that provides you with a sense of meaning and satisfaction, as well as financial stability, is a privilege, one that presumes agency and control over many aspects of our lives that – for many of us – we simply do not have.

Many of us do not have control over our work patterns, where we work or when we work. For many in traditional forms of employment this equates to new work rotas published one week in advance, and these weekly changes to the days and times of work make it next to impossible to plan for life outside of work. The increase or decrease in shifts at a whim and the extra time or overtime expected on demand add to the pressure.

Gig, freelance and consultancy work, sold to us as the ultimate form of agency and control in our career and work life, mean that many of us live a different working reality than the one our parents and grandparents knew. The fact is that this work is very often precarious and unpredictable. Many workers in these categories do not know if they will work next week, next month or next year. Contracts, if in place, are for short-term work that does not cover holidays, sick pay or pension contributions. While this may be touted as affording 'freedom', it also brings with it huge pressures for the worker – all while relieving the employer of the need to commit to their staff with the same commitment they demand in return.

Yes, the hourly rate can be higher in the gig economy, but so too are the risks. Payment terms are complex and challenging, with many large businesses taking 60–90 days to pay an invoice, and in some cases, they end up paying late, or not at all. A payment timeframe of two to three months impacts cash flow and ultimately your ability to earn a living wage.

That is not to mention the quid pro quo that exists for many workers, especially in creative fields, one that is seldom talked about publicly: the 'ask' to do things for exposure. The ask typically has a date, time and location attached, nearly always involving travel, and goes something like this:

'We don't have budget for this at the moment, but it would be great exposure for you to get involved.'

'The talk is only for one hour, the room will have a few of our senior stakeholders, we will make an introduction, we will put your details in our newsletter and on our website.'

The reality behind that ask is that you are expected to work for free.

So, why do we go to work in the first place? For some of us, going to work is about earning a wage to pay the bills and put food on the table. Work is not a choice; it is a necessity. For some, work is a place of refuge from the rest of their life. For others, work is about finding deep personal meaning; it is about a career and progression in that career.

Not everybody reading this will have the same experience or understanding of work, or careers, or life. Experiences change over time and as the seasons of our lives progress. In some seasons, more resilience, more innovation, more hours or more of anything is just not possible. You are going through the motions to get to the next season in life so that things might be a little easier. We will explore the seasons of life, and how they affect and influence our careers, later in this book.

If you do feel that you're going through the motions, be kind to yourself, do what you can. Take small steps. Ask for help. If you are in a season of life where it is possible to do more, or engage more, ask yourself whether this rhythm is one that you can sustain over the course of 40 years. If you choose to push and challenge yourself in your career now, is that preventing you from living the life you really want and need on a personal level? How long can you maintain this level of exertion?

So, whatever your reason for going to work, reconcile that for yourself. This will not necessarily make it easy, but it will likely make it easier. Please don't take this as advice that you should accept your situation without question. That is 100% not my intention. Rather, it is to avoid the trap of toxic positivity that lays the blame for your lack of agency at your door; this is not the case, and you are not to blame.

What must be highlighted is that we are all – at the individual, societal and organisational level – playing catch-up. How we engage with the world of work and how the world of work engages with us has changed. Our organisational policies and cultures, built on WEIRD logic, no longer serve us.

There are other possibilities available to us, we know that, but finding the space and time in our always-on culture to explore or consider those alternatives has been for many of us next to impossible. The hold these deeply ingrained and established ways of thinking have had on us often feel unshakable – that is until March 2020, when a global crisis illuminated new vistas of opportunity for work.

Covid-19 and the opportunity for change in crisis

Covid-19, the deadly virus that raged and ravished the globe beginning in 2020, forced us all to stop in a way never before seen, outside of wartime, in modern history. Government-mandated lockdowns required us to retreat into our homes and stay there to protect our lives, the lives of our loved ones and those in our communities.

Overnight, kitchen tables, bedrooms, hallways, garden sheds and spare rooms became impromptu offices. The boundaries that traditionally separated the world of paid work from the world of unpaid work collapsed, as the offices we once shared with our colleagues emptied. And we, along with our friends, our family, our animals, or alone, retreated to our homes to work, to live and to find meaning as the pandemic shadowed and dictated our circumstances.

We adjusted and adapted as we learned to live and work in the same space, something only 15% of the global workforce did pre-pandemic.[9] Zoom calls with professional dress from the waist up and pyjamas from the waist down became the norm. For parents with young children, re-enacting 'BBC Dad' – who appeared on live televised news around the world, with his child bursting into his office in the background – was a daily occurrence.

Long commutes were replaced with morning walks or a quiet breakfast. Families attempted a new type of juggle, one that required children to be taken care of and possibly home-schooled, while working full-time, as all day-care and education facilities shut down. Somehow, we managed.

After almost two years, as we rose from the ashes of the pandemic, something had shifted, something had changed. The old regimes, the pre-pandemic 'normal' no longer felt fit for the world we now occupied. Sure, there are parts we want and are glad to have back: hugs, close contact with loved ones, holding hands, nights out, time with friends and family, holidays, the spontaneous trip to the beach, birthday celebrations, road trips, a night away or a last-minute holiday. We each had our own bucket list: the things, the people and the parts we wanted back.

Most of us also had a deeper sense, a sense of what we *didn't* want – of the things that we didn't miss and that we simply did not want to return to.

Where working from home or remote working were once considered the preserve of the few, Covid revealed a different possibility. Pre-Covid, asking for flexible work patterns was considered a sign of weakness, an inability to manage, or a sign that you just weren't that interested in your career. In any case, visibility in the office and a culture of putting in long hours spoke to your commitment to your career and job over and above all else.

But overnight the pandemic taught us that none of this is reasonable. In fact, in an unwittingly anti-WEIRD experiment, that included the previously neglected 95%, it proved that most professional jobs can be done, brilliantly, from home, or indeed anywhere. It has shown us that we don't need to commute for two hours daily to do our jobs. In fact, it has shown that despite working from home during a life-threatening pandemic, many of us could still perform our jobs perfectly well and even excel at them thanks to the positive changes that working from home facilitated.

As this realisation dawned on us, we began to ask new questions, to think differently – and we resigned from our inflexible jobs in our millions. This global phenomenon has been coined the Great Resignation, yet I wonder whether this moment is the dawn of a reset in our relationship with and previous adherence to the old norms of work.

Are we leaving our jobs and breaking up with our careers because the pandemic forced us to stop, simultaneously confronting us with the harsh reality – one that we already knew but didn't have the time to think about – that the world of work we were living in was broken? Was Covid-19 the catalyst for many of us to start thinking about work and our careers as part of the greater whole of our lives? Is it possible that we are collectively redesigning what work means to us and through this collective action moving to demand a fairer, more equitable and more sustainable way of living and working?

Could work actually work for us?

We sit on the brink of a great opportunity – the opportunity to make work a healthy, sustainable space, one where we can finally strike a balance to live and work in harmony. This is a watershed moment in the history of work – an opportunity to think differently about how we work, where we work, why we work and for whom we work.

You deserve a career built on the pillars of meaning, respect, dignity and enjoyment. A career that respects your innate need to live life while working. Our realities, just like our careers, are multidimensional. Our careers are deeply interconnected, in ways we may not even realise, to the people we live with, the places we live in, our immediate families, our circle of friends and our tribe of people.

Yes, your career forms *part* of your identity, but it is not the entirety of your identity. Our careers, and the places that we perform them alongside our co-workers, need to respect the need for rest, relaxation and recreation if we are to thrive. The importance of meaning and the alignment of our values with our careers cannot be overestimated.

A career to love

We must shift how we think and talk about our career, if we are to create a career to love, one fit for life in the twenty-first century. That career should provide you with the best opportunity to be you, the chance to live and work as you thrive, flourish and progress in life and in work.

Building a career to love is not a new idea, but the one that we talk about here is different from a career built on passion. It is a contemporary concept emerging from data from the fields of vocational, work and career psychology. It is based on a representative cohort of the global population and is premised on the belief that our careers are contextual, dynamic and fluid.

Built on the pillars of dignity, respect, passion and compassion for yourself, for others and for the world we live in, it is a simple concept, one that places you, the person, at the heart of your career, and in so doing adheres fundamentally to the possibility that people, organisations and their teams can flourish and progress side by side. It is a new way of thinking, but Covid has shown us that we are more than capable of change. It speaks to the interconnected nature of the world we live in, the people we live with, and the lives we live. It's about connection to yourself, to others, to the wider society and acknowledges the ebb and flow of life as we journey through the various seasons. Transitions out of the paid workforce for rearing and caring are normalised. Time in unemployment or underemployment to look after your mental health and well-being are expected. The value in unpaid work is recognised.

A career to love is one where you feel that your world, your life and your career have meaning for you, for those around you and for the world you live in. It's about finding meaning in your career by finding your own definition of success, tapping into your innate human capacity to tell the story of your career, as you learn to tell, understand and follow your definition of success during the various seasons of your life.

To facilitate this movement, we'll take a deep dive into the myths that our world of work is built on, so that we can reset our relationship with any outdated logic that is likely driving our decision-making processes.

CHAPTER 2

Career Myths and the Stories We Tell Ourselves

Few tragedies can be more extensive than the stunting of life, few injustices deeper than the denial of opportunity to strive, or even to hope, by a limit imposed from without, but falsely identified as lying within.

– Stephen Jay Gould, *The Mismeasure of Man*[1]

The problem with myths is that we believe them

Stephen Jay Gould was a palaeontologist, a historian of science and an evolutionary biologist. Larger than life in many ways, he pushed the limits of his field of research, with his prolific writing focused on making scientific information accessible to all. A controversial character, he is often charged with forcing scientists to rethink deeply entrenched beliefs and to shift their focus away from pseudoscientific theories or myths and flawed data used to defend racism and other biases, and instead to focus on new and emerging information.

The above quote, taken from his book *The Mismeasure of Man*, brilliantly captures his critical perspective, and when applied to the career conundrum that a lot of us find ourselves in, it provides a point of connection. For so many of us, the cultural myths around work and careers are so domineering in our thought patterns that, instead of allowing us to consider the issues with the structures around us, they force us to point the finger of blame inward.

The truth is our society, culture and political systems generate stories; some of these are factual, while others are falsehoods or fabrications that come to be taken as truths – these are myths. Some of these myths are based upon outdated and disproven science, while others are created to serve a particular need, or are predicated upon findings taken entirely out of context.

Some myths are fun, others are less so; some are downright dangerous in their impact. It is to these last myths that we turn our attention, to examine how they have been rooted in our reality and impact how we make decisions.

Human storytellers and the creation of myths

Myths are, at their core, stories; they can often be immensely powerful stories which can be difficult to trace back to their origins, and even harder to uproot once they take hold. Myths are narratives which we, as humans, are susceptible to fabricating, weaving and believing. As humans, we are natural-born storytellers. We tell stories about ourselves for ourselves, but we also tell stories about other people for other people. These stories have the unique power to persuade, teach, motivate and anger ourselves and indeed others. Stories simultaneously hold the power to tap into our emotions, capture our imaginations and grab our attention.

In our modern world we communicate stories through a complex web of written, spoken and virtual media. So accustomed are we to telling and sharing stories in this way that we typically consider any story to be an edited narrative, spoken in public, written in books, acted on TV, shown in movies or created for social media. But long before we wrote stories down, in a time when the human mind was young, our ancestors crowded around open fires to hear tales of bravery and courage spoken from the mouths of shrewd hunters, brave gatherers and wise elders.

Unlike other animals, we lack the anatomical advantage of speed, agility, strength or fangs or claws to defend ourselves. We can't camouflage our skin to protect against dangerous predators. Instead, our distinctive human characteristic is our ability to extract information from our experience of the world around us and use it to solve issues arising from our restricted physical ability. As we do this, our improvisational intelligence kicks in and enables us to invent alternative ways to engage with complex problems. Our tribal ancestors started off with traps, nets, poisons and sharpened objects to stun, capture and kill otherwise out-of-reach prey and ended up with tools and strategies that enabled them to access food and resources that had been unobtainable.

Those generational stories told around campfires – of survival and narrow escape in a barren world, inhabited only by small nomadic groups – were educational and entertaining. The importance of telling and retelling these tales, accurate in all their intricate details, cannot be overestimated. In fact, such exchanges of information through stories were fundamental in building bonds between humans, through which we navigated challenging social settings and, ultimately, evolved as a species.

Since then, stories have continued to captivate generations of audiences, as they developed from oral epics to the written word, and eventually found their way onto screens. The power of those stories to transcend time, language and culture is profound and robust.

In short, our brain is hardwired for stories. Words crafted

into stories capture our hearts and minds, brains and emotions. Some we enjoy, others we don't, but universally, stories affect us; they influence our beliefs, alter our thoughts, shift our moods and impact our real-world decisions. Telling your story, having someone listen to it and really hear it, is a powerful and cathartic experience.

Telling myths about your career

When it comes to our careers, we both believe and tell stories all the time, we just tend not to think of it that way. Just as there are large-scale myths that structure how we think about the world of work around us, there are also smaller-scale, personal myths and stories we tell ourselves about how and why we work. As an individual, the last cover letter you wrote was an attempt to explain your why, your CV to tell your how, an application form to reveal the job-specific qualifications you have, while your interview communicated and convinced, through an oral story, that what you committed to paper is true.

In fact, so strong is the pull towards stories, particularly oral stories, that despite solid evidence from a host of academic fields that interviews are the least successful way to recruit for any role in any organisation, we persist with interviews. The qualities that are seen as favourable for interviews are not always qualities in common with the demands of the job. For example, interviews favour neurotypical extroverts regardless of the nature of the job role.

Recall, if you can, the last time you prepared for an interview and considered how to answer, 'What is your greatest weakness?' I bet you attempted to craft a story in which you, the heroic protagonist, either through feedback from colleagues, working with a coach, or self-reflection guided by personality assessments, identified an area of weakness, failure or potential improvement. Through dedication and rigorous attention, you have since worked to overcome that weakness. In that transition you have undergone a deep character change that makes you better now than you were before. This story not only curates you as a better person, it presents a story in which you are the best person for the job. Carefully rehearsed, as your story unfolds it informs the organisation of your capacity, capabilities and dedication to self-improvement, as well as the multiple benefits you would bring to the organisation.

Organisations also tell stories, through websites, on social media and, more formally, through yearly shareholder meetings, reports published, awards received and Glassdoor ratings. Generally, we call this 'branding' but in reality, it is the story the organisation tells to get you to work for them, to sell to you, or to invest in it.

Organisations use job specifications to tell the story of what they need from you, while performance reviews, dreaded or not, are the story of how you managed to negotiate your career story since your last review. Did you hit the right KPIs, or did you fall down somewhere else? Does the 'objective' performance review match the story you have in your head?

The point is that we all use stories to make sense of the world around us and to navigate our present while attempting to negotiate our future. We tell stories about our careers, and the way that we choose them. As we create, narrate and recall these stories, we craft them, interpreting and angling the facts, whether it's so that we appear resilient in the face of adversity, show a lack of weakness, or display how we have turned those very weaknesses into strengths.

One of the defining issues for most of us when it comes to assessing and understanding the problems with our careers is that we are told we should tell our career narratives in certain ways, and those ways are very often fundamentally flawed. They are rooted in myths about the world of work which we are told to believe, even if all the evidence says they are wrong. Just as the world of work is making us sick, so too is the information that we are using to make decisions about our careers. It is to these myths that we will now turn, and together we'll critically question how we got here and what we can do to reset our relationship with our careers.

The myth of a vocational calling

The idea that there is one true calling, vocation, or career out there for you, which you will uncover in a eureka moment is the first crazy myth that we must debunk. This is the idea that you will magically bump into the perfect career, and once that instantaneous connection is made, you will never work a day in your life again.

It is like winning the lotto or meeting your true love – one serendipitous movement between you and your career results in a perfect match. And yes, if it happens for you, it is magical, but for the majority of the working population that is not how it works.

So before we go any further let's deconstruct that myth, which requires some context involving St Augustine, Michelangelo and Marie Curie. Apart from the fact that each of them are well-known historical figures, they each also responded to a vocational calling – a strong, passionate voice, a sign that revealed what they should do with their 'one wild and precious life'.

St Augustine, a philosopher in his early career, changed roles to become a clergyman at the age of 32. After experiencing his calling, he went on to become one of the most influential thinkers in the Catholic Church. Michelangelo believed that his soul required him to paint and create, and while at times he wished to stop, doing so would have betrayed his calling. Marie Curie, who knew from an early age that she wanted to be a scientist, overcame every possible hardship, including poverty, hunger and the sexist social structures of her time to become a scientist and a Nobel Prize winner.

St Augustine, Michelangelo and Marie Curie each devoted their lives to a calling, a vocation. They had a deep-seated knowledge of their professional destiny. They did not have to think about what they would do for their career; rather it was bestowed upon them. Yes, their stories are inspirational and important, but they are also plagued by the vocation myth, the notion that choosing a career is a response to a calling that reveals your predetermined professional destiny.

The vocational myth, with strong religious undertones, suggests that discovering your career is something that passively occurs *to you* at a young age. The modern-day version of that myth is the belief that we each have a single talent, passion or ability recognised early in childhood, that once converted into a career provides the key to unlocking fulfilment.

Yet seldom do we consider this to be a peculiar question to ask a five-year-old: 'What do you want to be when you're grown up?' The notion that asking a child, who in most cases can't yet read, to project themselves forward into the role they intend to play in the adult labour market doesn't cost us a thought. Nor do we consider that their answer, depending on the response they get from influential adults, may become a self-fulling prophecy. We ask that same question repeatedly until children on the cusp of adulthood are told to choose a career.

We are suggesting that the career choice made in the earliest decades of your adult life is the right one for you for the remainder of that life. The very notion that those without a calling are in some way inferior to others is immensely damaging. Marie Curie, St Augustine and Michelangelo responded to a calling to careers that were of their time. Yes, Marie Curie paved a path into the sciences for women, but she did so also because her era made it possible. The 15-year-old Marie could never have experienced a calling to mine crypto, because it was not an option available to her, nor could Michelangelo appear on YouTube or St Augustine create AI.

In reality, the majority of us spend the better part of our careers searching for that sign, in an attempt to find our divine direction, often feeling underwhelmed by our achievements and overwhelmed by our actions. The world has set us up to believe that our career choices are something that reveal themselves. You yourself may hold these feelings deep down in your operating system, and if you do, again it is not your fault – which brings us to the modern education system and the role it plays in perpetuating this myth.

It is generally agreed that the core function of an education system and the polices upon which it is built is to help people navigate life and to (positively) support them as they make the transition from a student to a worker who contributes to society. In fact, the OECD Indicators Report on Education in 2022 highlights such educational outcomes as key indicators of a healthy and successful education system.[2] Which by extension suggests that career education should be, in theory, central to any education system. This might seem obvious, but is it the case?

In Ireland, the current provision for professionally qualified career guidance counsellors to support careers education is protected in legislation under the Education Act (1998) for 12–18-year-olds, with no formal service in primary schools. As of 2022, one guidance counsellor is considered adequate to support approximately 560 students in a mainstream post-primary school.[3] And while the provision of guidance within education varies from country to country, what you will find upon taking a deeper dive is that the delivery of careers education, much like in Ireland, is left to chance.

To put this in context, imagine if one of the STEM subjects (Science, Technology, Engineering and Maths), didn't form any direct part of the primary school curriculum, had a pupil–teacher ratio of 1:560 in post-primary, and had no specific requirement(s) at third level. Let's take maths as an example.

What if we said that one of the core functions of our education system is to ensure that every single child must be adept in multiplication, division, addition and subtraction, as well as trigonometry and geometry, by the end of their educational journey. But by some strange decision-making process, imagine that we had decided that it was up to individual primary schools if they should teach those skills or not, and if they did there would be no curricular support to do so, and it would be at best ad hoc. Additionally, imagine that we didn't scaffold the learning, but simply left learning maths to pure chance.

We did so in the hopes that one day by magical osmosis, all children would 'know' maths by the time they finish post-primary education. At the end of their second-level schooling, and without any formal instruction, we asked 17- and 18-year-old children to choose a specific aspect of university-level maths to study. Once chosen, they will study that subject for the next three or four years at least. If a young person told you that they were struggling or worried about their lack of formal maths education you would say, 'You'll be fine, don't worry about it, one day you'll figure it out.'

The idea sounds ludicrous because it is. But it is that exact logic that we apply to careers education and career choice, and when you can't find a meaningful career, the wider logic suggests there is something wrong with *you*. There is not. It is a myth that there is one vocation out there waiting for you. It is a myth that one day it will dawn on you. Careers education, like any other subject, is a skill that *must* be taught. Unfortunately for most of you reading this book, just like me, you were never taught these skills. If you have found the 'one' career for you, you are lucky. If you have not, your choice was left to chance, and that is not your fault.

The myth that personality testing helps you find the 'one' career for you

Closely linked to this notion of the 'one' is the idea that personality testing can help you find it. As we have established, career choices are amongst the most important choices that we make in our lives. The problem of choosing the 'right' career and finding a way to guide people through the confusion of that choice became apparent in the early years of psychology, vocational education and organisational psychology.

This led to a vein of scientific research that tasked itself with better understanding how people chose specific jobs, careers, roles or industries over others, and why some people were more successful than others in their chosen career path. In turn, this led to questions about a potential link between academic ability, innate interests, as well as individual difference when it came to career choice. This field of research was also interested in helping people, and organisations, find a fit between the individual and the job. We now refer to this area of research as the science of human personality.

Personality testing is complex, but boiled down to its simplest form, it is underpinned by the assumption that personality traits are highly stable over time and adhere to the belief as stated in 1890 by psychologist William James that 'by the age of 30, the character has set like a plaster, and will never soften again'. Using the stability of personality over time as a fundamental assumption, this field of research suggests it is possible, through the use of standardised questionaries, to find a perfect match between your personality and a single career.[4]

The science, if right, would be immensely helpful for individuals to navigate a path through the confusion of choosing one career from among the estimated 12,000 available, ultimately helping to avoid the disconnect currently experienced between people and careers. From an organisational perspective, it could also help organisations predict performance at work and cultural fit.

The father of 'vocational guidance' and author of the first personality assessments, Frank Parsons, working at the turn of the twentieth century, focused his life's work on establishing a scientific approach to career choice. To achieve this, he designed a 116-item questionnaire aimed at connecting the dots between personality and career fit. Parsons went into great detail in these questionnaires, which he outlines in his 1909 book *Choosing a Vocation*. Alongside the questionnaire, Parsons used the pseudoscience of phrenology in his studies, measuring the shape and size of a person's head to determine their ability and personality. Specific head shapes and sizes, he argued, were more animal-like, while others were more refined. He suggested that people with animal-shaped heads should be treated as such, while those with large, well-shaped and rounded heads were suited to more noble treatment, in professions such as engineering, law or accountancy.

This type of baseless pseudoscience seems ludicrous today. But while the personality tests available to us now don't measure head size and shape, they are built on and inherently influenced by the same principles as Parsons' model. It is also worth pointing out, albeit in a somewhat tongue-in-cheek manner, that the field of IQ testing has moved away from measuring the outside of the head and towards measuring what is inside the head instead – I wonder what the next generation will have to say about that?

Returning to our original point, the myth that personality remains stable over time has been remarkably persistent and continues to this day – many of us still believe that the vast complexity of human personality is capable of being reduced to a set of letters or numbers, usually four. Take the Myers-Briggs Type Indicator (MBTI) assessment, for example, based on 16 personality types. After taking the test, you are offered a dichotomous scaling of your personality, marking you as either introverted (I) or extroverted (E), intuitive (N) or sensing (S), thinking (T) or feeling (F), judging (J) or perceiving (P), different permutations of which highlight innate personality strengths and weaknesses.

By understanding your MBTI, the assessment suggests, it is possible to gain insight into your personality. This information in turn can help pave the way for personal and professional success, and specifically referencing career, workplace and leadership development. Every year it is taken by approximately 2 million people.

But most personality assessments, including MBTI, are not based on science. The exception to this rule may be the Big Five. The Big Five is a personality test referenced by some psychologists who, using scientific evidence, say that personality can be boiled down to five main traits represented by the acronym OCEAN: openness to experience, conscientiousness, extroversion, agreeableness and neuroticism. Each trait has a high and low score, representing two extremes.

These traits are each aligned with certain personality traits, believed to be stable over time. Someone high on the conscientious scale is a routine- and detail-driven person who spends time on tasks and thinks deeply, while their opposite, who is low on conscientiousness, dislikes routines and structures, procrastinates and fails to complete tasks to a high standard. Also, extreme extroversion is found opposite extreme introversion, though it is agreed that most people fall somewhere between the two extremes.

The Big Five is grounded in empirical research, with some results showing that your personality can influence your career, how well you do and how much money you make. Yet, as with other research presented as offering universal truths, it has many criticisms. Chief among them is the fact that studies replicated outside of the developed West do not show evidence of personality stability.

In general though, according to Benjamin Hardy, the organisational psychologist and author of *Personality Isn't Permanent*, personality tests are 'about as scientific as horoscopes'.[5] This is a pretty damning indictment of an industry that *Forbes* estimated to be worth upwards of $2 billion in 2021, and predicted to grow by 50% by 2028. It could be argued, and some have, that this is a headline-grabbing statement, but once you dig a little beneath the surface, you begin to see the truth in his argument.

Like the myths surrounding IQ, better and more advanced science tells us that personality traits are neither permanent nor stable. An *Annual Review of Psychology* study in 2019 found that evidence supporting personality stability across the lifespan is fragile and limited, and for the most part built on weak or indirect links based on small groups of participants.[6] This, as we know from WEIRD data, is deeply problematic. This newer, more complete research shows that, while some elements of personality remain stable across time and provide a baseline of sorts for understanding personality as a whole, the majority of traits are malleable and change as we mature and grow.

This myth of personality stability promotes both fixed-mindset thinking and the notion that some people with certain personalities are suited to certain roles while others with specific traits are not. The inherent suggestion that you cannot change, grow or develop in certain ways outside of your 'type' sorts people into boxes, and without education and support it can have a damaging impact. The fact that they are used widely in business to assign roles, assess performance and decide on promotions adds further gravity to the serious nature of this myth.

If you test poorly, yet achieve highly, you understand. Test anxiety plays a huge role in test performance, and negatively impacts 10–40 per cent of those sitting exams. Irish senator Lynn Ruane is a brilliant example of this. Leaving school at

15, she struggled academically. As a mature student she returned to full-time education, earning a degree from Trinity College Dublin, and at the time of writing, in 2022, she is reading for her master's degree. Lynn worked her way up through politics, and today she advocates for the under-represented and underprivileged in our society. Many test formats are simply not conducive to showing our true ability, as one size does not and cannot fit all.

Perhaps you have completed all the assessments, done the inventories and sat the test, but the job 'match' doesn't sit quite right. Or maybe you found your 'match' and love your job, but realise that the industry is deeply flawed and you have no possibility of progression – so while the match was made in heaven, the reality of it was not. This is not to suggest that these measures do not have a role; rather it points to the fact that the results of these tests do not uncover a single objective reality that points to the right career for you – the one that you should do for the rest of your life.

Myers-Briggs, 16PF, DISC and the like can play a role, but it should be one that comes with a cautionary note – they should be used to assist in making thoughtful and rational decisions, rather than acting as self-fulfilling prophecies.

Sarah's story

Take, for example, the client I worked with who headed up the financial division of a large multinational, and was doing a brilliant job. This client, whom we'll call Sarah, was taking part in a group team-building session using career-assessment tools to profile the team, encourage conversation and build trust, and as the session evolved, the facilitators, who also administered the test, showed a variety of perfect profiles for specific jobs.

Sarah was asked to share her profile with the room and it turned out that her profile was nothing like that of the 'perfect' CFO profile. In fact, her attention to detail and her ability to problem-solve and work with others were shown as poor, while her creativity and big-picture thinking were considered her strong points. The session shifted from a conversation intended to build a team and encourage trust to one about Sarah's ability to do the job she was already doing exceedingly well. Nothing else had changed except that she didn't match the profile.

The result was that she began to question her ability to do her job. She wondered if she was in the right job, and if there was something else out there that she might be better at. Given that she didn't 'match' the perfect profile, the questions her peers and colleagues asked her about her ability seemed to undermine her own belief in her capacity to do her job. Sarah left that job some months later, as the way others saw her and the way she viewed herself had shifted.

Admittedly, this is not just a story about the validity of these instruments; it is also about poor team training facilitation and a lack of ethical boundaries relating to confidentiality. Sarah's story is not, however, an unusual one. Career profiling and role matching is big business, and it is used for a variety of reasons beyond helping an individual to self-reflect so that she may make an informed decision.

The majority of personality assessments have no grounding in science, produce inconsistent, if not inaccurate, results, and could be identified as deeply flawed, if not meaningless in determining career choice.

It is better to think of personality, according to professor of psychology Brent Roberts, as a mix of stable and unstable traits that change over the course of our lives in response to how we experience life, typically leaning in the direction of positive outcomes.[7]

The myth of the linear career

The only place your career is linear is on your resumé. Yet there exists a very persuasive myth that your career, if you are to be successful, should have no gaps and show no sign of time out of paid employment, irrespective of the reason. The myth follows an 'age and stage' model, and goes something like this:

In your early 20s you should have secured a college education or completed a period of professional training, that initial professional choice determining your career path for the remainder of your working life.

In your 30s success is measured by your ability to scale the career ladder. During this particularly busy decade, men, who may become fathers, intensify their paid work patterns, while women, who may become mothers, either choose to stay out of the paid workforce, feel obliged to because of cultural expectations, or (as happened for decades) are forced to by legislation preventing married women from working in the paid workplace.

So this myth goes, in your 40s you are expected to have advanced the career ladder, in the same career you trained for in your 20s and, if you're capable, you are ready to move into a senior leadership role.

The expectation as you enter your 50s is progression to the most senior hierarchical ranks, including president, managing director, C-suite or partner. As you hit your late 50s you reconcile yourself to enter a phase of decline, both physical and cognitive. During this time, you start to check out and become focused on your retirement, a season of life during which you become entitled to rest, relaxation and time with your family.

The ensuing social code of organisational expectations and associated societal and family norms set in the 1950s has since then silently fuelled a social contract based on this linear notion of career progression. The length of time we stay in a job, the sequencing of paid and unpaid work, the lifespan of a skill and the amount of time we stay in the paid workforce before retirement have all changed. Shortened career sequences mean increases in the options and opportunities that shape our careers over time. This lack of predictability, alongside increased choices, has brought more uncertainty and hardships as the stories of our careers have become less age- and stage-related, as hierarchical progression, for the first time, became disassociated from chronological age.

To fit within the boundaries of this myth, we craft stories of resilience despite adversity, to show a lack of weaknesses, all while revealing how we have turned those very weaknesses into strengths. As we do this we attempt to cover any 'gaps' in that story. If you have taken time out of the paid workplace to care or rear, or look after your mental health, dread and fear run deep through the veins when prepping for the question, 'I noticed from your CV that you have a break in your working life. Can you tell us a little more about that, please?'

Answering honestly and declaring that your story is a human one, one that includes time out to have children, to rear your family, to care for a sick loved one, or to look after your mental health, sadly, for many organisations, doesn't fit the narrative of dedication to your career above all else.

McKinsey's Women in the Workplace Report 2020 showed startling statistics on the difficulties women face when returning to the workplace after a leave of absence, with one in three mothers reporting they were planning to downshift position or leave their role entirely.[8]

The Central Statistics Office of Ireland (2019) recorded large gaps between employment of women who have children and those who do not, with 88 per cent of women with no children being in employment in 2019 in comparison to 66.8 per cent of women with small children. The presence of a child had a much smaller effect for men, with an average 3 per cent point difference.[9] Research in the UK identified that almost half of women (43 per cent) are likely to return to work sooner than they would like after having their baby. Of these women, half of them stated it was due to fears surrounding job security.[10]

Fewer than a quarter of employed women in the US, 26 per cent in government jobs and 23 per cent in the private sector, according to the US Department of Labor, receive paid family leave through their employer.[11] Despite the US being one of the wealthiest countries in the world, the OECD identified the US as the only country to offer no national scheme for paid maternity leave. This lack of supports means one in four mothers in the USA returns to work two weeks after giving birth. Research has shown that extended maternal leave from the workplace has more adverse effects for women in more skilled jobs, as this absence leads to missed opportunities in career advancements, in comparison to women in lower-skilled jobs.[12]

Simply put, entry into and out of the paid workplace, for widely experienced and expected life events, does not seamlessly map onto the lean-in narrative.

That story has served nobody. This fundamental failure to understanding the (biologically determined) non-linear patterns of women's career stories means that 49.58 per cent of humanity experience their career through gaps – gaps in research, pay, representation, leadership and access to opportunity.

Male career stories offer a stark contrast to those of their mothers, sisters or female partners. The gaps that the women in their lives have in their careers are the very gaps through which they access opportunity.

By extension, just as the system denies women who are mothers permission to access paid work, it simultaneously denies men who are fathers permission to spend time with their children, to care for a sick loved one or to protect their mental health.

There is evidence of this at every level in every organisation, including in politics and sport. Bertie Ahern, the Irish taoiseach who was party to the successful peace talks in Northern Ireland, famously missed his mother's funeral to negotiate peace. On a very public level, when Cristiano Ronaldo and his partner birthed their twins in 2022, one of their babies was born an angel. Just 48 hours later, Ronaldo was back at work.[13]

A 2019 survey by an online parenting website revealed that one in five fathers missed the birth of their child due to work commitments that took them out of the country, or while making their way to the hospital from work got stuck in traffic.[14]

For the most part, these are not events that fathers want to miss, but the rules of work make it so, and such is the persuasive nature of those rules that they are seldom challenged.

The significant lack of uptake in policies that give equal access to paternity, parental and carers leave to men is a testament to this fact, this lack of entitlement to care and rear, while 'choosing' to intensify work patterns during this season of life. According to Ireland's Central Statistics Office in 2019, only 3.1 out of 100 men were paid their full salary for their two-week paternal leave in Ireland, which is significantly lower than the rate of fully paid maternity leave, which was 5.3 per 100 employees in the same year. Fully paid refers to the top-up of pay by an employer to the government allowance. The result: 45 per cent of fathers entitled to take up to two weeks of paternal leave did not claim it.[15]

Sweden, in direct contrast to this, was the first country to introduce non-gender-specific parental leave in 1974, with today each parent being entitled to 240 days of paid leave. Fathers account for 30 per cent of all taken paid parental leave in Sweden annually. In 2016, approximately 75 per cent of fathers took this leave.

If you are a woman in that dangerous age bracket of 30–45, then you make these decisions as you walk on career quicksand. Choosing to go for promotion shows intent and commitment, yet when you put yourself forward your capacity to 'do' the job is questioned, sometimes explicitly but most often implicitly. The subtle subscript reads, *What happens when you become a mother? Will you be able to travel, work long hours, remain visible, attend early and late meetings and also stay on top of your work at home?* Meanwhile, making the choice not to go for the promotion suggests that you're not serious about your career, and that your focus has shifted to motherhood.

The 'mommy track' is the modern term used to describe how mothers negotiate and are granted flexible working hours to suit the caring demands of raising a family, typically at the cost of further advancing in their career. Studies in northern European countries such as Denmark show how being a mother can have long-term effects on pay, with an average of a 20 per cent cut in earnings of women on this 'slow' career path.[16] According to the Bright Horizons Modern Family Index 2018, 41 per cent of employed Americans perceive working mothers to be less devoted to their paid work than to their children. The paradox deepens, however, as women who do not have children, or, increasingly, women who choose not to have children, are seen as overinvested in their career.[17]

Research shows that women in this category, irrespective of their choice to become a mother or not, suffer from this deeply ingrained bias. When one looks at the broader picture, little consideration is given to the women who choose not to go for promotion because they are using their lunchbreaks to attend fertility clinics, and their annual leave to undergo two anaesthetics, often within one month, to have egg harvesting and implantation surgery. Others carry a caring load that is so heavy that the added responsibility of a more senior role would be too great to carry. Still others, as they look up and forward, see burnt-out leaders and managers struggling to find a space where it is possible to live life and have a career.

Anyone who does not 'fit' the mould and the structures of the mould are perceived as opting out, not good enough, not having enough resilience, or presented as less than ambitious. The reality, however, is that the world of work, the spaces it takes place in, the times when it happens is linear and structured upon the needs of a very specific and tiny minority of the world's population.

This leads us to our next myth, one extremely closely linked to the idea that gender bias is on the decline or no longer exists.

The myth that gender and other biases don't exist (any more)

Unequivocally, this is wrong. Growing up we learn a strict social code about how we should perform our gender. The boxes we put people into are based on their biological sex, contain codes that prime their behaviour and their interactions with the world. From a careers perspective these codes prescribe how we perform our lives and temper the sense of entitlement we have to a career.

The field of neurosexism explores these deeply rooted gender-based beliefs within our society. While some of us have convinced ourselves that this reality does not exist, in our lives, our organisations, or our culture, it absolutely does.

Much of our prevailing logic relies upon a deeply held and silent belief, that women and men have biologically different brains, that result in innate gender-specific behaviours and emotional capabilities. It exists around us, and once you see it, it is hard to unsee. The next time you are out shopping, check out the different slogans on the tops for our girls and boys. Girls' clothing, alongside the pink embellishment, are emblazoned with phrases that promote gratitude, positivity, kindness and plenty of smiles. Boys' clothing boasts words that focus on bravery, self-confidence, leadership and rebellion – 'here comes trouble' chief amongst them.

The extension of this myth is that girls are more caring or nurturing than boys, while 'boys are naturally better at maths than girls', or 'girls are better with languages'. Emerging research in neuroscience and neuropsychology tells us there is no scientific support for the persuasive story that binds gender and the ability to care and rear or to the ability to learn languages or maths. We are conditioned to believe these myths, and sadly all too often we do.

One story illustrates this point beautifully. During World War II, the first lines of computer code were written to calculate the trajectory of ballistics more accurately. This work was done by six mathematicians hired by the military, each of whom tirelessly calculated the angle soldiers should fire their weapons based on their distance from a target, weather conditions and a range of other factors. This work was time-consuming and laborious but central to the war effort.

To reduce the time investment, two scientists developed a machine with the capacity to calculate ballistics trajectories faster, and the first computer, called ENIAC, was born. Using that computer without any instructions or manuals, they figured out how to accurately create ballistics trajectories. In doing so, they created programming languages and manuals.

The two scientists, both male, rightly received great attention for their pioneering work. However, the original six programmers and the others who followed during the war were almost all women. The women who created the language integral to the outputs of the computer were written into the margins of history. When the war ended and men returned home, the first computer programmers and coders in the world were relieved of their duties. While two of the original six continued to work in the tech space, four of them did not. Jean Bartik went on to lead the development of computer storage and memory, and Betty Holberton designed the first software application. Today, almost 100 years later, most coders and programmers worldwide are gendered male, but this is not due to their genetic predisposition as natural coders and programmers. It is because we have created socially constructed narratives that are gendered male.

From a biological perspective there are specific anatomical factors at play that make us distinct, but none of those factors relates to the above examples. Science tells us our specific anatomy means that we have different functions when it comes to conceiving, birthing and feeding a baby, but once a baby is born, nurture and love are not gender-specific, and the two are most certainly not mutually exclusive.

Some women are more natural carers than some men, yet there are also some men who feel more natural as carers than some women. While men and women have different biological capacities when it comes to childbearing there is no evidence that those biological capacities determine who should leave home to engage in paid work and who should stay at home to do unpaid work, nor should it determine the type of paid work either should do.

The arising narrative denies both men and women permission to thrive, flourish and progress at work, but more important, in life while at work. Yes, perhaps some men are better than women at maths, but also some women are better than men at maths. In our workplaces, it presents itself as the alignment of leadership with men and caring with women. This has unimaginable impacts for women who are mothers and men who are fathers, as discussed above. But the impact does not stop there.

A 2021 meta-analysis looking at the link between sexuality

and pay disparity between 2012 and 2020 in Europe, North America and Australia found persistence of earnings penalties for gay men, lesbian women, bisexual men and bisexual women, across each geographic location, despite the bolstering of anti-discrimination policies at national and organisational levels. For example, men who are openly homosexual pay a wage penalty estimated at 16 per cent compared to similar heterosexual men, while women who identify as lesbians earn between 9 and 20 per cent more than heterosexual women, depending on where they live in the global West. And lesbian women are still paid less than straight men.[18]

The mind-boggling complexity of the pay hierarchy deepens because men in single-sex relationships earn 11 per cent less than men in traditional heteronormative couples, while women in single-sex relationships earn 8 per cent less than those men, and overall earn more than women in heteronormative relationships. The data for transgender or non-binary sexual orientations is not yet conclusively available, but sadly it does not look promising.

Where neurodiversity intersects, the pay penalty deepens, with workers diagnosed with additional needs penalised at every step of the way. For those who make it into an organisation, they are more likely to suffer underemployment and a significant pay penalty.

Each International Women's Day, we lament the gender pay gap by organising events to tell the story of women and other supposed minorities who survive the corporate world. We show how organisations support real change and attack the numbers. But that story is a convenient one. It hides the reality that according to the World Economic Forum, it will take 132 years, or almost six generations, to close the gender pay gap.[19]

While the gap between female and male workplace participation has narrowed, with a representation of 46 per cent and 54 per cent, respectively, the result of a workplace built on the myth of the ideal worker remains prevalent. The CSO Gender Balance in Business 2021 report for Ireland revealed that only 13 per cent of Irish CEOs are women, one in seven boards of directors have a female chair, and only 30 per cent of all senior executives are women.[20] This begs the question, if labour force participation is all but equal, how can such discrepancies exist between the numbers of women in the workforce and those in leadership positions?

The answer is not found in education or performance: research published in the journal *Frontiers in Psychology* shows that female and male co-workers consistently perform as well as each other in both education and work. Nor is the answer legislative in nature, given the raft of protections in place. Additionally, most workplaces now have flexibility policies, and people have access to remote work.[21]

The answer, it appears, is that our morals and ethics do not always follow the law. Despite more education, high performance standards and new ways of organising work, the twenty-first-century workplace still manages to produce and reproduce old forms of inequality, bias and exclusion that feeds rather than challenges the gender pay gap.

What is the issue? And more importantly, what can we do about it? For a start, our response should not involve a call for more resilience, harder work or more leaning in by women or those from other under-represented demographics. In fact, we know that people from these groups who do reach leadership roles are just as likely to be professionally excellent, and perhaps more so, as to obtain these roles they will have overcome brilliance bias, leadership bias and gender bias. Nor should it rely on deepening binaries that position men and women in a gender war.

So rather than necessitating for these exceptional groups to do more of anything, it's time for a new narrative, one that doesn't demand ideals from anyone. It's time to challenge conventional wisdom that no longer serves us.

The myth of the work–life balance

The idea of a work–life balance (or WLB for short) has dominated the discourse around careers, work and well-being for years. Yet universal agreement on what WLB is is hard to find. There are, however, some commonalities, with most of us thinking of it as an equation of sorts – one that involves divvying up time into slots allocated for work, with others dedicated to non-work activities such as time with family, friends, hobbies, healthcare, socialising, rest and recovery. Once WLB is reached, the story goes, you can declare your status as a successfully 'balanced' twenty-first-century adult.

First off, the narrative perpetuating the myth is confusing. Despite the glorification of WLB, and the apparent simplicity of the concept, the facts reveal a very different picture.

The word 'work' in work–life refers exclusively to paid work outside the home, while the 'life' in work–life refers to non-work activities such as spending time with family, friends, hobbies, socialising, rest and recuperation. Paid work occurs in a place and space outside of the home for 39 hours each week – for some weeks more but seldom, if ever, less.

This type of paid work is performed by a character we know well – the unencumbered 'ideal worker' who is available to stay late, is 'always on' and willing to respond to calls and emails on demand. As you might recall, the ideal worker is also open to travel or to relocate for work, to socialise after hours and prioritises career success over family or leisure time.

The space to account for the unpaid work that makes paid work possible remains written into the margins of the WLB narrative – the cooking, the cleaning, the shopping, the washing, the ironing, the millions of jobs that must be done to make work and life possible. These 'things' are seldom accounted for when we talk about WLB, and therefore fail to fit into the box that is either work or life.

Sitting in that same elusive, hard-to-define 'neither box space' is care for children and/or care for older family members. Yet all this work must be done, either by someone who stays at home, most often a woman, wife and mother, or it is outsourced. While the concept of WLB may have served some when men left home to do work and came home to do life, while women stayed at home to do both work and life – that is no longer true.

This notion that men do paid work and women do unpaid work, and that all homes are made up of heterosexual couples with children, is outdated. The reality could not be more different. According to the CSO, 63.7 per cent of Irish women in 2020 were active in the paid workforce, 70.2 per cent of two-parent families were also dual-income homes, 47.8 per cent of one-parent homes are in the workforce, and 36 per cent of families in Ireland are defined as nuclear – that is, made up of heterosexual married parents and children living together without grandparents. The remainder of households, and therefore the majority, live in homes that are 'non-traditional'. Single-parent families are, according to research, the least satisfied with their WLB, while married men in paid work manage WLB better than married women in paid work.

These figures are reflected in an OECD 2020 Work–life Balance report across 29 countries, including Ireland. The report shows that the average satisfaction with WLB is below 8 out of 10 in all OECD countries, with an average satisfaction level of 6.9 out of 10.[22] CSO figures for 2021 in Ireland show similar results. When that data is segregated to account for gender and full-time employment the same figures show women and girls, aged over 16, consistently work longer hours, in paid and unpaid work combined, than men. Men are more likely to feel satisfied with their WLB and spend on average 45 minutes more per day on leisure activities than women. Women and girls, on the other hand, have less daily time available for 'balance' and are more likely to feel work–

life conflict. But digging a little deeper into the data, it becomes apparent that while some men feel a greater sense of WLB than women, the majority do not feel significantly more satisfied.[23]

While workplace flexibility in terms of temporal and spatial qualities has brought some 'balance' to the notion of WLB in theory, the reality is again different. How we think about flexibility and how we use it to achieve WLB is deeply gendered. Research by the European Group for Organisational Studies shows that when mothers or carers ask for and are granted flexible working arrangements, there are expectations about how it 'should' be used. The 'extra' time is bargained for, and expected to be used, to cover school or crèche drop-offs and pick-ups, to deal with unexpected illness, to manage medical appointments and to take care of the unpaid work necessary to run a home. This flexibility often takes the form of reduced hours across the day or week, during a specific season of life, typically motherhood.[24]

The same research shows that men with similar care responsibilities who avail of flexibility are expected to use it in a more limited and event-focused way. Men are expected to intensify their work hours and improve their performance after becoming a father, using flexibility occasionally to attend matches, for sports days or to go to a school play. The result: women during years of parenting and caring are expected to 'opt out', while men during those same years are expected to 'opt in', to achieve WLB.

The long-term outcomes of such cultural and social expectations about WLB are shared in the Harvard Happiness Study. This, the longest-running global study on adult development, traces life outcomes for graduates of Harvard from 1938 to the present. The study found that the greatest end-of-life regret of professional men was their overcommitment to work when they had a young family and the lack of time spent investing in their relationships.[25]

But what about the rest of the workforce? What about the 1.4 million single people living in Ireland with no children? What about the professionals and managers who do not have children or other caring responsibilities? What about their equal and important need for WLB? While the overall rhetoric of WLB has changed over the past 20 years, similar unfair expectations about how single professionals should perform WLB and avail of flexibility exists. The belief that solo-living colleagues have free time in abundance and are therefore 'expected' to use flexibility to work late or to cover increased flexibility for colleagues with high care demands is not spoken about.

Research shows that when single workers bargain for flexibility the legitimacy of their 'ask' is often questioned.[26] The lack of understanding for the financial burden experienced and the sole responsibility for all unpaid work resting on their shoulders is typically overlooked. While organisational rewards are often career progression and development opportunities not afforded to parents working flexibly, this does not adequately address the same deeply human needs of solo-living colleagues.

The overall picture is clear: a very high number of men and women, from all life stages, irrespective of personal circumstances, or gender, are unhappy with their experience of WLB. The reality is that WLB in its current guise works for vanishingly few people. It denies everyone, men and women alike, the permission to live their life in a way that works for them.

The myth that with age comes cognitive and career decline

A significant myth around age sits silently in the margins of the story of our working lives and careers. Referred to as ageism, it is the broad belief that with age comes decline, and therefore older workers are often considered less willing, less interested and/or less capable than younger colleagues. Research from the *Journal of Applied Social Psychology* shows that this myth is accompanied by the belief that creativity, problem-solving and the ability to learn new things and adapt decrease as we age.[27]

Given that workers aged 45–74 globally are the fastest-growing demographic in our workplaces, with women aged 50 and over accounting for the largest segment within that demographic, we must address the myths that drive ageism as part of the wider conversation about work and careers.[28]

So what are the beliefs that drive this myth, and what can we do to debunk them?

First off, we do not fully understand the entire picture of ageing and cognitive ability in healthy adults. Advances in fMRI imaging have, however, advanced what we know well beyond the commonly held belief that with age comes decay. Research based on this data reveals that adults have two distinct types of intelligence: fluid and crystallised. Fluid intelligence is our ability to problem-solve quickly and to respond innovatively to novel experiences. Crystallised intelligence, on the other hand, is the ability to use historical information alongside our skills and knowledge acquired over time and apply those learnings in creative, innovative and practical ways. Fluid intelligence starts to decline in healthy adults during their late 20s, a universal experience of humanity. Crystallised intelligence for healthy adults continues to develop and accumulate across the lifespan, showing no signs of age-related decay. In practice this means that across our adult life, while healthy, irrespective of age, we each enter peaks, plateaus and canyons in our ability.[29]

In addition, fMRI imaging shows that people of all ages have an equal ability to be creative and innovative, to learn new things, lead groups, problem-solve and engage in their work; they just rely on different cognitive functions to do so. By staying in the workforce, trying new things and learning new information, ageing workers are in fact shown to maintain fluid intelligence while increasing crystallised intelligence. This ebb and flow of maintenance and increase in fluid and crystallised intelligence is linked to higher levels of emotional intelligence, empathy and compassion.[30]

The idea that cognitive decline comes with age is a myth that research has completely debunked, but sadly the wider social narrative has not yet caught up. The result: ageism in our workplaces is rife due to lack of understanding and education. In particular, older workers are often viewed as less tech savvy and computer literate than their younger counterparts. While the tech knowledge gap that once existed has declined to the point of disappearance, there remains a perception that it still exists.

Older workers can be as tech savvy and computer literate as any other worker. And if you needed any further evidence, take note of the rise of the 'Grandinfluencer'. 'Grandinfluencers' are the hordes of tech-savvy older adults using social media to smash these age-related myths. Take Iris Apfel, the 101-year-old with 2.4 million followers on Instagram. She launched her career in the world of social media and fashion at the age of 84. In the past 16 years, her idiosyncratic look of oversized glasses and accessories, paired with flea market finds and high fashion has seen her skyrocket to fame in an industry notorious for ageism. Since then, she has collaborated with H&M, Macy's and Bergdorf Goodman. Not to mention that she signed a contract with one of the world's largest model agencies at the age of 97. Age aside, influencers like Apfel are fierce, brilliant and as tech savvy and social media literate as someone a quarter their age.

Which brings us to the next aspect of this myth, namely that career success happens around age 30, but if it is going to happen at all it will absolutely be before you turn 40. The yearly '30 under 30' lists get plenty of attention, but what about the '50 over 50' who are making their mark and taking their place in the world of work and finding their career space? There are plenty of role models who achieved career or business success after 40.

Vera Wang designed her first bridal dress at 40. Actors Viola Davis and Octavia Spencer both achieved critical acclaim in their 40s. Kathryn Bigelow was the first female director in history to win an Academy Award. She did so at age 57. Mary Robinson and Mary McAleese both became presidents of Ireland in their mid-40s, while Ursula von der Leyen became the first woman president of the European Commission in 2019, at the age of 61.

These stories represent success in its most complete form, a type of career success that happens as part of the ebb and flow of life, not instead of it. The next step is to move the dial beyond research and broaden its scope in the wider conversation about making work a better place for everyone. Reviewing the relevance of mandatory, statutory and contractual obligations to retire in the public and civil service in Ireland, and other parts of the world, provides a starting point.

Normalising job design to explicitly make provision for all, including people as they age and experience ill health, is a further step. Using age-diverse imagery in our wider media coverage is also vital. As part of our business education programmes, we must normalise conversations about leadership and management that speak to ability, experience and potential based on ability not age.

As a 42-year-old woman on the cusp of 'old' by the prevailing standards, I believe that I am *not* old. I may be older, yes, but old? No way. I steadfastly refuse the notion that my career and life journey is one of decline and stagnation due to age. I counter with the belief, backed by knowledge, that as I enter this phase of my life I am fuelled and filled with potential, creativity and ambition. I look to others leading the way for inspiration, and I rely on the research to inform my inspiration. From this vantage point, with the myth of age and cognitive decline critically questioned, it is possible to see increasing chronological age as a number to celebrate rather than a limiter of potential.

The myth that creativity is the reserve of the few

Aligning creativity with babies and children in the first instance, we hold a belief that creativity, innovation and play is the preserve of the young or 'the creatives' – the artists, painters, jewellers, singers, dancers, songwriters, sculptors, musicians and poets who illuminate our worlds and soothe our senses with beautiful prose, sculptures, music, clothes, jewellery and paintings. And while we are led to believe that creativity belongs exclusively to these groups, the reality is that we are *each* wired for creativity. Creativity is an integral part of our DNA and it is central to our evolution. We are all 'creatives' – but we express that creativity in different ways.

The expression of personal creativity might be shown in the way we dress or displayed through a unique thought process. Equally it could be the ability to develop and deliver an argument, the capacity to join the dots between previously disparate pieces of information or the talent to convert complex data into easy-to-access information. In some instances, it is the ability to be curious and ask questions, and to follow a single crumb of information that begins something new.

Creativity is without doubt about art, music and aesthetics, but it is equally about how we apply our imagination in a way that changes how we (and others) experience or view the world around us. We know and recognise the importance of creativity and innovation, and yet as children grow into adults and learn to navigate the world, many are scolded for daydreaming, for their overactive imaginations, or for having their head in the clouds. On the other hand, the down-to-earth, rational, no-nonsense person is praised.

Examples of these myths include the belief, for example, that we use only 10 per cent of our brains, that there are different types of learning styles based on brain type, and that men use one side of their brains and women use both. Chief amongst these neuromyths is the belief that as humans we are either right- or left-brained. This is quite simply not true.

The world of work and careers does not escape this narrative, with the result being that certain types of career are privileged over others. The accompanying suggestion privileges certain careers and suggests that there are some careers more suited to left- versus right-brained people, a widely held belief. Right-brainers, the creatives of our world, are the emotional and intuitive abstract thinkers, driven by their imagination. From within this field of thought, right-brainers are more suited to careers in the arts, literature and theatre, tending to occupy lower-paying roles. Left-brainers, on the other hand, are the analytical and logical types who are practical with strong verbal and mathematical abilities. Left-brainers are suited to high-paying careers in science, technology, maths and engineering.

As a result, many are advised to avoid careers in creative industries. Again, you are familiar with the story: 'Don't be an artist, you'll never make a living from it. You are good with numbers, what about engineering or computers?'

'Acting, that's a nice hobby. What will you do for a living? Maybe you would consider teaching or law? You're great with language.'

'Media and journalism? You have to be well connected to get a job in that area. It's hard to get a mortgage doing a job like that.'

Creative jobs are presented as the the nice to haves, but the one you *should* want, the one that results in a 'good' career, whatever that means, are for those with fully operational left brains. This thinking is supported by a widely held belief that different parts of the brain are responsible for specific cognitive functions. Creatives are subsequently siloed into functions separate from other 'real' work.

This wider social and cultural narrative, according to research in this area, brings sudden slumps in the development of our creativity, particularly as children enter formal education and navigate their way through the system. While there is debate surrounding the exact timing and depth of these slumps, the literature agrees that where creativity is encouraged through education the slumps are less severe and children remain more curious, and ultimately more creative. Pause to think about your own educational experience, or that of a child you know, and it's likely you recognise these transitions.[31]

Moving from pre-school through to post-primary, the curriculum slowly but surely shifts away from the more creative endeavours of free play, art, singing and dancing to focus on the more 'serious' subjects, including languages, engineering, maths and the sciences.

For the most part, music, art, drama, sport and dance are positioned on the sidelines of 'real education'. Creative subjects, it appears from this logic, do not adequately prepare our children to transition from full-time education into the world of work. After all, the core function of our education systems is to prepare us and our children for the future of work. More about that in a moment, but first let's return to creativity.

This field of thought, both in practice and theory, is the result of neuromythology, an emerging field of research that is actively dispelling misconceptions about brain research using advanced fMRI imaging and technology that did not previously exist. While the research upon which this thinking is based was considered legitimate when it was carried out, it has since been discounted time and again – and yet the logic has remained persuasive.

Evidence from the European-wide Human Brain Project and the Human Connectome Project in the US, alongside expansive research from *Frontiers in Psychology*, repeatedly produce evidence, based on the best of modern-day technology, to the contrary.[32] Yet these myths persist, to our detriment and unwittingly impact how we make choices in the world of work and about our careers.

The myths we believe shape our realities

The seven myths we explored are but some of the myths that impact our everyday logic and determine the decisions we make. The purpose of this chapter is to trigger you to thinking about those myths and how they have impacted your career to date.

Primarily, it is about arming you with the information to challenge these myths when and where you see them impacting yourself, your family, colleagues, friends or team members. The prevailing social narrative must shift away from home versus work, life versus career, male versus female, parent versus non-parent and put the needs of all humans alike at its core.

We live in a time of great possibility. If there are no rules and if we have a new working reality, the question becomes: 'What could we do if we accepted that careers (either paid or unpaid) do not have a gender; that careers do not have a race, nor are they determined by your sexual preference; that careers do not demand each of us to be neurotypical and able-bodied.' The same is true of leadership roles, the capacity to care for others or to parent a child. How we conduct our careers, leadership and our unpaid work roles are socially constructed entities, based on data that evolved from biased research.

While it is bleak, examining these myths in their social, political and cultural context is vital, for it is within them that we make decisions about our careers. Curiously, questioning these myths reveals the story written into the margins of our decision-making process, the silent persuasive rules that we don't see and therefore don't consider in our decision-making process. We each accept them as how things are, but deep down, we feel frustrated and overwhelmed because the lived experience is one of no matter how hard we lean in, or how hard we try, we just don't seem to be doing enough of the right thing to get to the next level.

These silent and coercive rules exist in the ether, fundamentally impacting our decision-making process, and tempering our agency. These myths, which can often manifest as rules, dictate organisational and individuals' sense of entitlement as to what work–life balance is and how they are entitled to perform it. That very sense of entitlement is so deeply embedded within the fabric of how, where and why we 'do work and life' that without question, we have internalised and normalised them.

In the next chapter we will look at the real-world impacts of these myths upon your own career, and how they can result in a working life that is sustainable and healthy – or unsustainable and detrimental to your personal life and your very health.

CHAPTER 3

Unsustainable Careers – Do You Have One?

While The Clash were famously asking the question of whether they should stay in or leave a relationship, every time I hear the lyrics of 'Should I Stay or Should I Go', they remind me of my early career. I remained in a toxic job because I loved what I was doing. I had long realised that I needed to go but I was plagued by indecision. And as I spent more and more time in that job it slowly became apparent that my indecision was making me sick, and that loving the function of my role was no longer enough.

But while in that job, a strange thing happened: despite being really good in my job, my confidence fell off a cliff edge and I became paralysed in deciding if I should stay or go. My worst fears drove me to stay, as I feared that I would never get another job, that if I left I wouldn't get a reference, and that I really wasn't good enough at my job anyway. And just when I needed my logical, rational brain to kick into action, it failed me. I froze.

I knew what I needed to do to change and I knew how to do it. I did it for others all day every day, but making the decision to move from thought to action and initiate change for myself filled me with fear. It brought with it what I now understand to be a complex, deceptive and unnerving cognitive and psychological process made up of catalytic events. For some, these events make the move easy. Others, like me, end up in a near constant state of paralysis.

Why is this the case? Why do we continue on the same path, in unsustainable careers, even when it makes more sense to leave?

Why do our careers punish us rather than set us free?

At the time I was in that job I didn't have the language for what I was feeling or experiencing. The job was permanent, pensionable, secure and carried a decent salary. It was close to my friends and family, in the area where I lived, and the opportunity to progress was not limited. In theory, it ticked all the boxes of a 'good job'.

But my body told me that this was not a good job for me.

Likely, you know these signs: tense shoulders, tired despite eight hours' sleep, that feeling of never getting to the end of a to-do list. Living and working towards the weekend to get a rest, but the rest never feels full. Frayed nerves and tested patience as you get to the end of another day or week. Sunday night brings worry and anxiety, and then those feelings gradually start to creep into Saturday.

Either not using your annual leave or taking it only to get sick as soon as you take it is another tell-tale sign, the outcome being that rather than relaxing you use your holiday time to recover. As the end of your leave approaches you start to feel well again, and just as you do your thoughts turn to the unanswered emails clogging up your inbox, the ones that kept coming (with CCs from the same people – over and over) even though they knew you were away. You can't help but think of the heavy workload that awaits you upon your return.

Perhaps you continuously experience moments that trigger you to want change in how, why, where and when we work

– you know those moments, the ones when you promise that you are leaving the organisation, switching jobs or transferring teams if office politics kills your project, internal management shuffles stifle your progression or your boss steals your work one more time. Few careers remain untouched by office politics, management decisions, stress, burnout or other events that propel you towards change.

Yet taking that final step into the abyss is hard (really, really hard), even when your core values, sense of fairness and fundamental preferences are challenged – not to mention when your work and career are making you unwell.

Research by renowned professor of organisational psychology Herminia Ibarra on the link between career endurability and identity suggests that we find it difficult to break free from the choices we made in the past that led to our present, even if that change would bring about a different, perhaps better, future. That research suggests that we can feel unable to make any decision about our working identity as it is so entrenched in our daily activities and deeply connected to important others in our lives. Changing any one part of this risks changing others, and for most of us, trying to figure out the efficacy of the risk over the win is enough to paralyse us and put us into a state of permanent pause. Put simply, we are not only attached to our work and careers, we are emotionally attached to the people and places connected with our careers and work lives. This emotional connection has the habit of complicating and confusing our decision-making process, thereby rendering us almost, if not totally, unable to make any decisions.

Catastrophic thinking – when the worst things happen in your head

When faced with a task while enduring ongoing stress about something that is important in life, such as your career, relationships and work, catastrophic thinking often kicks in. Catastrophic thinking is irrational and illogical thinking based on doomsday outcomes. This happens to us all on occasion, and when it does it is inevitably accompanied by an increase in anxiety and a decrease in the ability to make good decisions.

During that early phase of my career, I played out catastrophic thinking in the following way: 'If I leave this job, I will never get another one. I live too far away from jobs that suit my qualifications. If I leave this job I'll be unemployed and then I won't be able to pay my share of the mortgage. Alan will leave me, and I'll never meet anyone else.'

When I finally did leave, none of those things happened. In fact, my worst nightmares played out only in my head, leading to a sense of what academics call liminality, a suspended state, an almost altered reality in which my past, present and future selves were independent of one another. None of these 'parts' were yet connected or tethered in a way that made sense. As I battled to figure out 'who am I' in my career and work, a framework I used, like many of us, to derive personal meaning and social connection from, I felt lost. Previously, I used that defining framework to make decisions about, and set priorities for, other important parts of my life.

Those facts sat in the ether as I realised that I was not the architect of that framework, the one that framed my career and by extension impacted my life. That felt really confusing, and alongside this confusion sat the fundamental knowledge that my earlier ways of understanding myself no longer served me; in fact they failed me to the point where I was unable to make any change. Existing in that liminal state, a space where multiple possible selves co-existed, alongside a version of myself that was shaken, made the decision to make change, any type of change, really difficult.

The path forward was about as clear as mud. Conventional advice to 'stick it out', or to 'think about the pros of the job' deepened the denial and led to a questioning of my experience. Career-change strategies led by questions like `Who am I?', or `What one thing should I do?' felt far from helpful; instead they made an already difficult choice feel even more difficult.

So, like others who are trapped in a role, an environment or a career where meaning and fulfilment are no longer present, I stayed. The profound awareness of the problem alongside a growing dissatisfaction in work, life and career wasn't enough.

So why did I stay, and why do you stay?

What motivates you to stay?

It depends! Some of us use our wages to motivate or reward ourselves. Online shopping patterns show an increase in shopping for luxury items on Mondays and Thursdays between 8 p.m. and 9 p.m. Thursday-night shopping 'treats' are your reward for getting through the week, while purchases on Monday serve to motivate.

We may also reward ourselves with an evening glass of wine to unwind before bed while scrolling social media to find an answer to 'what is wrong', only to feel much worse for that scroll. All it has managed to do is reconfirm your worst suspicions – 'others' are in fact managing to 'have it all'. The accompanying feeling of guilt is intensely felt, because on paper you too have the dream: a well-paying job, a place to call home, the opportunity to travel, the means to have fun and a network of people you call family and friends. And for all of this you are grateful, but you 'should' be more grateful, less stressed and definitely happier.

But you are not.

Maybe you would be happier, or even more successful, if you were up at 5 a.m. for a sea swim, constantly striving for the top position at work, cooking for yourself and travelling to luxury locations with ease, all while dressed immaculately. If you become a mother, the onus is on you to bounce back to your pre-baby shape within weeks. Not to mention the requirement to find time for hobbies, dates, friends and volunteering. If you are not managing this with a smile, well, then you are not managing.

This level of pressure in terms of how you perform in your life and your career isn't sustainable for anyone, yet alone everyone. The idea that if you are not grinding 24/7 then you are not successful is pervasive, and a notion that we cannot sustain. And yet, we are motivated to stay in those roles, to remain in our jobs and persist in our careers. We find reasons everywhere to remain.

Psychologists suggest this is a result of our tendency to seek out information that supports decisions or choices that we have already made. A form of selective memory, referred to as confirmation bias, it narrows our frame of reference and anchors us to the choices previously made when our experience was different. This manifests as misjudging or missing altogether important facts or details in our careers, such as missing relevant opportunities, focusing on the wrong areas and ultimately toxic positivity.

Have we reached our tipping point?

Collectively, trying to self-manage and function in these types of unsustainable careers and workplaces has pushed us to a tipping point, a point of no return, that magic moment in time when a small but significant minority takes a stand, moves to action and, with that movement, brings lasting change. In his book *The Tipping Point*, Malcolm Gladwell suggests that these crucial moments are triggered by an event that births a collective realisation: that the time for change has come, as the old world no longer serves us.[1]

Perhaps Covid has brought us to that tipping point, where we collectively take a stand and express our long-held feelings that we are no longer willing to work in jobs that consume our identities and see us live to work rather than work to live. Covid gave us food for thought. It slowed the pace of the race to the point where we could think while talking. Long commutes, global travel, face-to-face meetings, working 9 to 6 and many other previously necessary demands of the pre-Covid workplace ended abruptly, and were replaced with flexibility, remote working and a different way of doing things. We learned, overnight, to cope, to manage and to shift our perceptions.

This collective tipping point was dubbed the Great Resignation by Anthony Klotz, organisational psychologist at Texas A&M University, who describes the phenomenon of people in developed economies who quit their jobs en masse.[2] According to the US Department of Statistics, 47 million Americans voluntarily left their jobs in 2021, and research by the Pew Institute in the US reported that 63 per cent of workers who left their job in 2021 did so mainly due to a lack of opportunity to progress in the workplace, while 45 per cent stated a lack of flexibility in working hours, particularly a lack of choice on when to put these hours in, as a deciding factor in quitting their job. Lack of flexibility and poor childcare options were highly correlated to leaving the workplace, with 48 per cent of respondents giving this as a determining factor.[3] Canada, Europe and Australia show similar trends.

With these statistics in mind, we must remember that some workers who chose to leave did so immediately after the worst of the pandemic had dissipated, and that these figures include those in jobs who would have left them earlier if it weren't for Covid-19. Once relative stability in the labour market returned, they left, and those figures are a natural and expected spillover from near static employment turnover during Covid-19.

The question remains: Why did so many others choose to voluntarily leave their roles in the wake of the pandemic? Professor Isabell Welpe of the TUM School of Management in Munich, an expert contributor to the World Economic Forum, recently conducted research into why people are leaving their jobs in such large numbers. The most significant factor in that decision was where employers expressed a preference for or demanded a full-time return to the physical office. Research participants cited the impact the return to the office would have on their ability to balance work and life. Importantly, the ability to have work–life balance (WLB) was cited as a significant contributing factor across multiple demographics within the workplace, and not only among working mothers – research shows that nearly everyone wants flexibility with the 'where' of work.[4]

Research by the Pew Research Centre and the MIT Sloan School of Management agree that, while pay is a contributing factor in employee turnover, pay, when fair, ranks only 16th in terms of reasons for leaving a job. Expected full-time return to the office coupled with a lack of flexibility in work patterns and an overall poor response to Covid-19 rank highest in influencing the intention to quit. Lack of clear career progression opportunities, failure to fairly recognise individual-level performance and contributions, and toxic cultures follow very closely.[5]

For those who are unhappy at work, even if they're not living pay cheque to pay cheque, their unhappiness takes its toll on the rest of their life. The result is that, even if it means a pay decrease, many look to make work and career changes that would have been unimaginable pre-pandemic. Most of those who choose to leave work still want to work, but not at any, or indeed all, costs.

Why career self-knowledge is power

Knowing how to find work that you enjoy and to self-manage your career is a skill, not an innate ability. As such, the skill of career management is learned and requires education. We know from Chapter 2 that the myth that your career will suddenly unveil itself to you has by some distorted logic meant that we are not educated to choose, understand or manage our careers as they unfold across the course of our lives.

Countries that supply career education across all levels of education and afford the opportunity for working adults to freely access career professionals show positive overall workplace well-being outcomes. Nordic countries implement a welfare model that aims to ensure maximum participation and healthy well-being for those seeking employment, those in a current job and even those moving towards retirement. Finland has established a network of local drop-in 'career' centres for people under 30, to access free advice on careers, education and everyday life. In 2018, a survey was conducted among service users to analyse the effects of the initiative, and 85 per cent of people using the service reported that their confidence in landing a job improved greatly upon accessing the services. Not only did this service provide users with new employment opportunities, but 86 per cent of respondents reported that the programme gave them a clearer view of their future career path.[6]

The Uberisation of careers and the Platform Revolution

When you think about your career, or careers in general, you may not align it with Uber or indeed a revolution. But the current career landscape has changed so dramatically in the past two decades, driven by platform technology businesses like Uber, that it is almost unrecognisable. The so-called Platform Revolution, which coincided with the Great Recession, signalled a rupture in the organisation of work and careers. While self-employment, freelance work and consultancy were already in existence at that point, the gig economy was new.

The gig economy refers specifically to work obtained by people using platform technology – think Deliveroo cyclist or Uber driver, where an algorithm decides who, what, when or *if* you work. Platform work, and the algorithm driving it, is based on a trio of needs: the platform itself, the customer and you as a worker. As a worker you work on demand, and in many cases, you are not guaranteed a specific amount of work on a daily, weekly or monthly basis.

When you work, you are paid by the hour as a subcontractor, and therefore do not have the right to any form of paid leave. While it is true that you have more flexibility and autonomy over your time, it is also true that this disembeds workers from the organisation and the protections a career within an organisation once meant.

Gig work has increased in breadth in recent years, and is now frequently used to refer to anyone who works via a platform, as a freelancer, consultant or someone who is self-employed. Key to this type of employment is the fact that *some* gig workers are in a position to set their own fee by the hour, day, week or month, and have the freedom (at least in theory) to work their own hours. In exchange for this freedom, you pay your own taxes, make your own pension contributions and cover your holidays and/or sick leave.

The gig economy has pros and cons, as with any change or development in how, why or where we do anything. For some workers, gig work provides steady, rewarding and well-paid work; for others it is precarious, unstable and badly paid.

This new type of work relationship affords some individual workers autonomy, agency and flexibility over their career and work lives. For others, typically those in more precarious employment, it brings with it a lack of agency. The safety net attached to the traditional employment relationship is sacrificed for the increased hourly rate, and increased flexibility.

It is interesting to note that research published in the *Annual Review of Sociology* in 2020 found that while there were some gig workers who were entirely dependent upon platforms for work, the majority were in fact not, as they held down full-time jobs outside of the gig economy and used these platforms to earn extra money.[7] This is interesting, as the research does not dig into the detail of *why* these workers are taking on extra work. Does it reflect a need to earn extra money as their full-time job does not cover the cost of living, or is it a side hustle, or a means to gain experience and traction in a new career venture?

Depending on which lens you view it through, the gig economy may be an entrepreneurial incubator or a digital cage. Either way, it points to the reality that we each need to understand the knowledge, skills and ability required to self-manage our careers in this career and work landscape.

The end of job security?

Where once jobs and careers were always attached to an organisation with the security of permanency and a pension forming part of the social contract, the world of work no longer offers this sense of security and stability to many. Work patterns, tenure and the associated careers now follow a different tempo. According to the European Union Labour Force Survey and Eurofound, job tenure (i.e. the average length of time a person stays in the same job in the same organisation) is now just shy of 10 years – a dramatic change from the 'one job for life' of previous generations.[8] According to the Bureau of Labour Statistics, the figure in the US is 4.1 years. Senior workers, in terms of age and position, are more likely to remain in the same organisation than younger, more junior workers.[9]

As the landscape has changed, so too have the patterns of careers. Careers have shifted from organisational to within, between and across organisations and industries. Alongside this, many careers have shifted outside of organisations entirely to form the 'gig economy'. Many gig workers are knowledge providers who supply their services to organisations on a freelance or contract basis.

The advent of the gig economy has placed the responsibility for owning and managing your career decidedly at the door of the individual. It is now up to individuals to choose a career path and engage with extra learning in order to progress up the ladder.

This involves learning the key knowledge and skills that prepare you to work in the present and to remain employed into the future. Understanding the necessity, or not, to upskill, reskill and retrain while working, which is central to your employability, is key. It also requires the ability to negotiate contracts, benefits, perks and pay, not to mention the next step in your career. Specific education in these key skills is central to achieving this. Understanding where the gaps exist in your current skillset, how your industry is developing, and where the opportunities of tomorrow lie, are vital to avoid those gaps becoming problems. Maintaining your employability is indeed a big challenge, and one most of us face as we attempt to gain and maintain our ability to stay employed with or without employer support.

These contemporary trends have created a plethora of career paths. Today, O*NET in the US, run by the US Department of Labor and the European Skills, Competences, Qualifications and Occupations classification offer a matching service between people and over 20,000 jobs within 900 job families.[10] Considering the huge number of jobs available to choose from and the extensive list of career categories, the notion that it is possible to choose the one that you will remain in for the rest of your working life seems unnecessarily restrictive.

A fresh perspective – a sustainable career

In response to all of this, it's clear that we need a fresh perspective on contemporary careers, and we need it urgently. We need one that's multidimensional so that it takes into account the natural rhythms of life, and acknowledges that careers are non-normative. Even those that do conform to the 'norm' are conditioned to do so, often at the expense of their personal life.

Such a narrow approach fails to capture the essence of the individual. Flawed as a concept, it fails to account for the deeply interconnected relationship between work, career and life. It doesn't capture the potential that occurs in your subjective experience and understanding of ambition and success over time. If you are anything like me, your definition of success has changed fundamentally over the course of your life. What was important at 20 may no longer be the most important measure of success in your life now. Likewise, what is important now may pale into insignificance in years to come.

We need a framework that is not just flexible, but that engenders a sense of entitlement to have a career while living a life. By sense of entitlement, I do not refer to the phenomenon where some cohorts believe themselves to be entitled to certain privileges in the world of work, and in their careers, over others. Sense of entitlement, in this context, is the belief that people, just like you and me, have a fundamental right to earn a living while living life. It is where we work in the understanding that burnout, stress and overwhelm related to work and career success are wrong, and where it happens we will, together, do our utmost to stop it. In short, this feeling of disconnect between our lives and our careers should be the exception and not the rule.

Organisations need to ask themselves: Are we greedy? Are we living off the ambitions of people who can conform to the notion of the ideal worker? Are we asking some of our talented workers to do the job of two or three people and at the same time expecting them to maintain a healthy work–life balance? Do we have some people who can live up to those expectations and others who can't, and what are the consequences for that person when we behave in a way that is not sustainable towards the individual?

The shift to remote working in 2020 due to the Covid-19 pandemic saw an increase in burnout levels of those working from home. A report by Gallup entitled 'The Wellbeing-Engagement Paradox of 2020' demonstrated how working from home was associated with both higher levels of engagement and intensified emotions of stress and worry.[11] The fear of losing employment during unprecedented Covid times was the main factor in an increase in work stress. Personal well-being was affected by everyday tasks, whether it be children demanding your attention or health fears surrounding Covid, and it was ultimately this disconnect between engagement and well-being that led to higher levels of burnout among those working from home. The rise of terms such as *karo jisatsu*, a phenomenon known in Japan as 'death by overwork', is indicative of such issues. Such is the prevalence of this that the World Health Organization estimated that 745,000 deaths globally from stroke and heart disease in 2016 came as a result of long working hours and stress.[12]

This book – and the concept of a sustainable career – do not claim to 'fix' this phenomenon, nor does it claim to 'fix' you – and just for clarity, 'fix' gets inverted commas, as you do not need to be fixed. You are not broken. What is broken is a system built around myths about work, life and career that demand that you perform complex contortions to conform to the demands of a world of work that no longer serves us.

PART TWO

Reset: The Courage to Create New Alternatives

CHAPTER 4

Breaking Patterns – Exploring Alternatives

Where patterns are broken, new worlds emerge.
– Tuli Kupferberg

As a child of the 1980s who grew up in the 1990s, I wanted to be a lawyer. This desire was based on my love of *Ally McBeal* and a fascination with the lives that independent working women led. I was so enamoured by the career story of a successful lawyer that I transplanted my teenage dreams onto the life of Ally. There was no real thought and no major decision, just a hunch that opened the story of my paid work.

But my dream, to which I had attached my identity, collided with reality, and within three months of starting my studies, I realised that Ally McBeal's career story was not to be mine. I was not cut out for the life of a lawyer. So strong was the narrative created in that show that I based my future identity on it, and when the actualities of my life collided with my future, and it misaligned, I became confused, upset and scared. My future career, the one I had deeply identified with, and which had become so integral to my identity, was shredded.

My family had been proud of my initial choice and, frankly, I liked the idea of the lifestyle it afforded my future self.

Rewriting that story was hard, and learning to tell a new story was even harder. Making the decision to tell others that I was no longer going to be a lawyer, in short, was really difficult. This was compounded by the fact that I didn't know what my new story would be. What story was I going to tell myself? More importantly, what would I tell others? I really struggled to make the right choice.

Somehow, a career I hadn't yet started, or even fully trained for, grew to be intrinsic to my identity, so much so that at the age of 21 I was afraid I would never know what I wanted to do, and that I would fail to achieve anything. With the luck of having patient parents, I took a new path and moved into education, specifically careers education, and from that into psychology. And, eventually, my career story emerged, at the intersection of these three professions.

I know that if I had clung to the notion that I could be a real-life Ally McBeal, I may not have written this book. I made three career choices that didn't suit me, I stayed in one job way too long and I eventually, on the cusp of my fourth decade, made a choice that worked for me. In other words, experience, failure, success, hardship, financial difficulties, disappointment, enjoyment, education, learnings, creativity, a thick skin and openness to new experience led me to here.

The skills I learned, the people I met and the knowledge I gained equipped me with the tools I needed to transition into owning my own business. I could not have chosen the job I now do, that of a career and work psychologist, when I set out on my career journey at 17, because this job did not exist. In 10 years, I may want to do something entirely different; this may be possible, and it may not. This is how the world of work, that we now live in, operates.

My point is, there is no magic formula to answering the deceptively simple question – 'What do I want to be when I grow up?' or 'What do I want to do with the rest of my life?'

We each want straight answers, someone to say 'you should do this or that'. But in a world where change is the new permanent, old ways of thinking about novel circumstances do not work.

Our desire for help is understandable. We are all inclined to want help. Life is busy, if not hectic. All day, every day, we make decisions and we suffer from decision fatigue – not to mention the fear of making the wrong decision, and the judgement that may go along with that. Taking account of the fact, as explored in Chapter 2, that our careers-based education is left to chance, we simply are not equipped with the skills to manage our careers.

However, if you don't have an active role in designing your career, someone else will do it for you, and frankly you may not like their version. So it is at this point that we turn towards the idea of a sustainable career. What is it and, more importantly, how do you get one?

What is a sustainable career?

In the spirit of transparency, there is no definitive answer to this. I appreciate that this may not be what you were expecting at this point, but this book is not about giving you simple answers to questions that only you can answer. Nor is it about false hope or vague promises. It is about supplying the tools, equipping you with the courage and knowledge to design a sustainable career for your present and future self. What is clear, however, is that it is possible for you to have a sustainable career once you are happy to get into the nitty gritty!

The notion of a sustainable career is a contemporary one, emerging from the academic research of Ans De Vos and Beatrice I.J.M. van der Heijden, two highly respected contributors to the fields of career development. Through work on the concept of a sustainable career they speak to the multidimensional and complex human phenomenon that we each experience as we attempt to live life, while having a career.

Using this broader, more context-rich lens, a sustainable career focuses on you, the individual, at the centre of your career, as you are influenced and moulded by your social, political, cultural and economic context. Importantly, it respects the lived experience of us all, meaning work and home are not considered to be separate entities – from this perspective they are in fact deeply interconnected. This means we must rid ourselves of the notion that our careers are devoid of context. That is simply not true.

Instead, we must build our psychological mobility as we equip ourselves to navigate our careers as they develop in the context of the opportunities and constraints presented to us in the broader context of life. Psychological mobility is an attitude to change, one that is prepared to cross traditional career boundaries or to break free of the myths that once underpinned our decision-making process. The contemporary context in which we live out our careers reflects the changes in how we live our lives.

Where once career progression and success was measured by hierarchical progression through an organisation, that decision is no longer straightforward. The plethora of career options we face presents us with decisions to accept or quit a job, to work part-time or flexibly, to become self-employed or solo-employed, to stay in our current career or develop into another one.

Alternatively, it might present itself as a period of unemployment, underemployment or overemployment. Whatever the choices you are faced with, psychological mobility recognises that there is no 'one' true self, but multiple selves that co-exist, and it is these multiple selves that are the drivers of our career decisions.

A sustainable career is, therefore, not defined as a predictable and unfolding sequence of paid employment across the lifespan, as in traditional models; rather it respects the non-sequential, non-linear ebb and flow of the various seasons of life. In so doing, it acknowledges that as we go through life we transition within and between a variety of seasons of life during which transferable skills are earned and learned. A sustainable career implies explicitly, and without apology, that all skills are valuable and transferable, not just the ones that have traditionally been accepted by and valued by the market.

Importantly, true well-being and wellness sit in the centrefold of a sustainable career. Careful consideration is given to actions, or inactions, in the present, so that you engage with a meaningful career in the present, without compromising your ability to do so in your future due to burnout or poor health.

Can I have a sustainable career?

Absolutely, you can have a sustainable career – with one caveat: you must be willing to begin your journey from a place of curiosity and courage, all the while asking questions of yourself and others. Your focus is to explore all the possible answers that work, or are most likely to work, for you during this season of life. For that reason, a sustainable career does not come with an algorithm. It does not provide you with formulated or formulaic answers. Instead, a sustainable career is a practical framework through which you learn the skills to craft the story of your career.

It focuses on you, the expert in your career, as you attempt to build a career that satisfies you personally and professionally, while providing you with the hope that you can continue in that career into your future. It considers what has gone before and what is happening now and uses the totality of that information to educate your future.

Importantly, a sustainable career does not pretend that work and all other non-work parts of life exist as distinct themes that run through your career, parallel and never meeting. It does not suggest that you need to be more resilient, qualified, visible or more of anything. Nor does it suggest that you need to be less visible, less forward, less candid or less of anything.

A sustainable career focuses on the sweet spot in which your career, your life and your work collide, collapse and connect with each other in and through you, all the while acknowledging the different meanings attached to work and careers during different seasons of life.

In essence, a sustainable career exists at the very point where each of your '&s' intersect, the messy grey space in and through which you live life, and access your career. It is to these '&s', your '&s', that we will now turn.

A sustainable career – the many aspects of who you are

For many, as the research outlined in Chapters 1 and 2 shows, the compartmentalisation of life and work has meant working as though we didn't have a life and living life as though we didn't work – and who can blame us? This normalised behaviour results in a moulding and conditioning of us, from the start of our working lives, as ideal workers. You could even argue that this process starts before we begin our working lives, during our childhood, as we absorb the messages and ideologies that surround us in our environments.

And when we begin to dissect it, it makes intuitive sense that when we go to work it doesn't mean we stop thinking about life. And just because we leave work to turn our attention to life doesn't mean that we stop talking about or thinking about work. This is particularly so since we have started to work from home, or in coffee shops, when we're working in meeting hubs and in locations not traditionally dedicated to work.

We have begun to think about our lives, our careers and our work as intersecting with one another, rather than operating in separate domains. In so doing we acknowledge that these parts of life overlap, and as they cross in and through one another, they're not neatly compartmentalised into siloed sets of hours or days.

In essence, it is the realisation that you are the sum of your '&s', and that these '&s' change, alternate and develop in terms of the position they play in your decision-making process across the course of your life. Your '&s' are unique to you, together forming and unfolding to provide information about what a sustainable career is for you. Exploring your '&s' involves learning to acknowledge each one, understand the role they play in your overall life, and to respect each one in their entirety for the space they occupy. It does not mean you will always like the story of your '&s' but it is in that story that your reality becomes apparent.

Familiarising yourself with each of your '&s' is therefore essential to understanding what a sustainable career means to you. Likely, this is not something you do frequently, yet it is hugely important. The value lies in placing all of the information that impacts and tempers your decision-making process in one location. Likely, this is not something you do frequently, yet it is hugely important.

What are your '&s'?

Beware, this is a deceptively simple question that requires you to permit yourself to fully acknowledge all of the roles you play in life and what each of your '&s' represents in the wider context of life.

Invariably, when I do this exercise with clients or in organisations I am asked the following question: 'Is this my personal or professional "&s"?' This is a reflection of the deeply ingrained and falsely held belief that personal and professional lives are separate. I always answer with the same response, 'It is up to you' – so the same response stands here. Ideally, as you engage with this Pause for 60 you will at the same time write down both your personal and professional '&s', but if it is more comfortable for you to take two Pause for 60s, dedicating one to professional and one to personal, that also works. So, as suggested, 'it is up to you' . . .

What is, however, of deep significance is that as you write you activate your Permission Mindset – that is permission to yourself, from yourself to write freely, and without denying yourself the opportunity to write the words, phrases, sentences or ideas that come into your head. There are *no* right or wrong answers, there are only *your* answers.

Acknowledge that as you kick off this process you might feel discombobulated. In reality, we tend not to reflect too much on the reality of our multiple selves, but trust the process.

Are you a professional?
& single?
& a partner?
& a carer?
& a parent?
& a friend?
& a daughter?
& a sister?
& a sports addict?
& a podcast listener?
& a fashion addict?
& a lover of the arts?
& a writer?
& an artist?
& a runner?
& a meditator?
& a problem solver?

& a leader?
& find it hard to say no?
& a daydreamer?
& a personal taxi driver to your kids?
& fed up?
& really tired?
& struggling with your health – either physical or mental?
& searching for a sustainable career?
& loving life . . .

The above is a list of '&s', and while it is long, it is only a guide containing simple samples to trigger your thought process. It is not exhaustive, nor is it intended to represent *your* list of '&s'. The number on your list and the meaning and feelings attached to each of your '&s' is not only representative of you, it is unique to you. Some lists are short and complex, others are long but simple, while others are both intricate and long. The number of '&s' or the complexity attached is not the point here; you are instead seeking to understand the broad spectrum of dynamic and interconnected experiences at play across your entire life.

So with that in mind let's start your first Pause for 60.

Pause for 60

What are your '&s'? Pause for 60, pick up your pen and begin to write (in a notebook that makes you smile when you look at it). Jot down, draw a mind map or create a list – whatever works for you – as you do include each of your '&s'. Remember, there are no right or wrong answers and there is definitely no marks out of 10 for the perfect list. Rather, there is your list, the list of your &s, the ones that are important and meaningful for you.

Set your timer and begin to write.

At the end of your 60 seconds drop your pen and pause.

Read through what you have written, and reflect on what you have written. As you consider your '&s' ask yourself, 'What have I left out?'

Have you left out the fact that you are a rainbow parent, or the parent of a baby born sleeping? What about your mental health and well-being? Do you live with depression or anxiety? Do you manage chronic pain? Are you dealing with grief?

Your '&s' are the whole of you. Each forms a part of who you are in life, at work and in your career.

Pause for 60

Pause for 60 again. This time, give yourself permission to acknowledge all of your '&s', including the ones that might be harder to put on paper. It's likely that your page looks less than perfect, but your '&s' represent the messy points at which each of your '&s' intersect.

If this was perfect, life would be easy all of the time. This is the kaleidoscope through which you experience your life, your work and your career. This, my dear reader, is reality.

Identity covering and your career

Excluding any of your '&s' leads to a lack of authenticity, the feeling that you are not being true to yourself. By extension, when you do not feel that you are being true to yourself, it can feel challenging to *be* your true self. Hiding or concealing integral parts of your identity consumes considerable energy and results in a feeling of isolation. This is referred to as identity covering, or concealing a core aspect of yourself, either consciously or unconsciously. You do so to avoid making others feel uncomfortable, or to lessen attention to a given characteristic that might otherwise be detrimental to your career or work progression.

For example, wearing a power suit to appear more masculine, not using a walking aid for mobility issues, fathers not applying for flexible work to facilitate childcare. In some instances, it is not bringing a plus one to work events as a member of the LGBTQ+ community, deciding not to wear religious clothing or concealing your age. On the other hand it is the decision to not make an issue of a joke that is aimed at race, gender, age, sexual orientation, citizenship, political affiliation, religious beliefs or disability.[1]

Deloitte, in a 2022 study on inclusion and diversity at work, focused on the impact of covering at work, found that 61 per cent of all workers covered part of their identity at work in some way. Identity covering was more prevalent in historically underrepresented groups in the workplace. But significantly, 45 per cent of straight white men also reported identity covering.[2]

Identity covering is different from, and not to be confused with, lying or manipulation. The intention of identity covering, specifically in the workplace, is not to downplay or conceal pieces of your identity for untoward purposes, but rather is a result of trying to blend in with the majority, so that a core aspect of your identity does not block access to opportunity or progression.

This does not mean that you should share all of your '&s' at work, or at the start of an interview, but acknowledging them and understanding them as part of your overall professional and personal identity, and decision-making framework, is vital. What you are attempting to do, in this exercise, is to acknowledge everything that you do in all the different parts of life. By understanding and naming your '&s', you begin to process their role and impact in your life.

You might be interested to see my list of '&s'.

It is edited, as this is not about sharing everything with others; it is about understanding for yourself.

I'm a mother of four,

& a partner

& an individual

& a business owner

& a professional

& a deeply ambitious woman

& I often lack confidence

& I struggle with procrastination

& I love big picture thinking but I find the detail a real struggle

& I believe that we can make the world of work a better place for everyone

& I have developed in my career four times

& I hate domestic chores like cleaning but I love to cook and bake

& I get overwhelmed when I take on more than I can do

& I love to spend time by myself, reading and listening to music.

So what are yours? Flesh them out, and as you write them down, think about how they cross over and intersect with each other. They're all impactful in your career and in your decision-making process around your career, work and personal life, so name them.

The five Ws of a sustainable career

As you grow to understand your '&s' as they impact on your life and career, learning how to navigate and negotiate them in a way that works for you during this season of life is fundamental. Using the five W's: the what, where, when, who and why of life, work and career helps you to do this.

To write the story of your sustainable career you will learn to place your five Ws central to your decision-making process. And there are times when achieving agency is not possible, times when what is happening in your career, life or work is simply outside your control, and your choices are limited. It may not be clear why this is happening, but the sustainable career framework positions you to understand it and determine when it is the right time to move on.

Previous career research tended to explore work and home as two separate and distinct spaces, one where some people had careers in return for paid work, and the other where people (statistically women) stayed at home to perform unpaid work. The evolution of the workplace to include more women in paid work roles outside of the home has confronted both men and women with the responsibilities associated with work and home life.

Adding to this, there is little being done to address the rising imbalance of power in the relationship between organisations and the individual workers. In some organisations, workers are often expected to fit into the spaces and places that the organisation needs, rather than fulfilling their own aspirations. Busy on the rollercoaster of life, we write this off as luck or as a career that just 'happens'.

You know exactly what I mean if, as you read this, you can think of job interviews you went to because you were expected to, and choosing not to go forward would look like you weren't interested, but in truth you didn't want to go for the role. If you have struggled to understand the gap between what the policy says and what happens in the organisation, and yet feel you can't speak up, you also know what I mean. If you have felt the need to stay late to show interest even if that meant you were missing an important life event, you feel what this means in your bones. If you went for the job interview, got the promotion and really didn't want to take it but knew that if you didn't you would never get the chance again, you know the story.

Work and home are not separate – they are in fact deeply interconnected. This means we must orient ourselves towards the notion of sustainable careers – ones in which actions now do not cause burnout later.[3] The 5W's of work are about ensuring that our actions in the present are not so intense that they prevent us from working into the future. That may manifest as burnout, or other mental or physical health issues.

A sustainable career is not defined by the predictable and unfolding sequence of paid employment across the lifespan; rather it respects the transferable skills earned and learned during the times in life when someone needs to leave the paid workforce. A sustainable career implies explicitly, and without apology, that all skills are valuable and transferable, not just the ones that have traditionally been accepted by and valued by the market.

A sustainable career is one that develops over time so that it meets your needs in the present, without compromising your ability to engage with meaningful and fulfilling paid work into your future. Theoretically, crafting a sustainable career involves meeting your present needs while preserving your future ability to work and simultaneously endeavouring to achieve this without compromising the ability of future generations to meet their needs.

The length of time we stay in a job, the sequencing of paid and unpaid work, the lifespan of a skill and the amount of time we stay in the paid workforce before retirement have all changed. Shortened career sequences mean increases in the options and opportunities that shape our careers over time.

This speaks to the shift in the relationship between you as a worker and your organisation. At one time, the space in which you performed your career was relatively straightforward – organisations and institutions were the official providers of career paths and provided the space within which you crafted your career story. For the most part, careers in this social space were considered as separate from life.

As the world of work rapidly globalised in the late twentieth and into the twenty-first century, the boundaries between work and life began to collapse inwards, and as this happened the level of interdependency between work and life increased at an exponential pace. A multigenerational workforce, the growing prevalence of dual-income and dual-career families, not to mention the ubiquity of technology and the pace at which it advances, have each contributed to a sprawling expansion of the stage upon which you can perform that career. Careers are seldom contained within a single employment setting within a single industry over time; instead, careers are a mosaic of experiences, learnings and movements occurring within an increasingly complex environment.

A sustainable career

As we have discussed already, careers are complicated. They're a collection of experiences of objective and subjective evaluations occurring over time within an increasingly diverse environment. This rich variety of sequences of experience makes up your career. As we'll explore further in a later chapter, sometimes they involve positive career shocks, other times the shocks are negative. These episodes can be demotivating or rewarding.

But the complexity of our world means that there are many opportunities for individuals to make choices in line with what they want to do, and why they want to do it. That's where the notion of a sustainable career plays a vital part. We know that what looks like a really successful or satisfying career to many is one that makes money. We also know that many people feel that their career is their entire identity, and that a shock, one that negatively impacts this career and the identity associated with it, can have lasting effects on the individual.

Take, for example, the overly ambitious young graduate. Putting in long hours and continuously knocking it out of the park is accepted and rewarded by organisations, and this can push people to the brink, putting long-term success at risk.

There are points in our careers when we might need to just do a job – to work for survival alone. Your list of '&s' help you to understand what point in your career you are currently at. In these moments of survival it is not about upskilling, reskilling or retraining, it's about getting through the job in order to be able to leave work on time, and to start work at a reasonable time so that you can take care of other things outside of work. During these times when you are going through the motions you may be missing out on career progression or development opportunities. This feels wrong because it is wrong. Up until this point in your career, you have worked hard and proven yourself as more than a capable professional, who deserves to get that progression or development. You know this moment of survival will pass and you will regain your space, but if you are passed over without understanding, as often happens from within the traditional careers model, the long term career impact can be massive. On the other hand, a sustainable career respects these natural ebbs and flow in life, and consciulay commits to avoiding these scenarios.

The aim of a sustainable career is to build, create, and develop rather than deplete and destroy. For these reasons, the sustainable career looks at how you as an individual can avoid the health problems that come with traditionally defined careers, while strongly inviting organisations to look at their role in this.

Sustainable careers build and create and develop rather than deplete or destroy. They are about conservation and renewal. They are about responding to individuals and the world outside an organisation. They are about dynamic engagement with people, about expecting and understanding that life and work happen hand in hand, that this cycle of events and decisions that determine when, how, where and why people work is important. As a concept, sustainability gives us permission to break the notion that only those who conform to the standards of the ideal worker, either feel, or have an entitlement to a career. It acknowledges the fact that people's careers don't always occur in a straight line.

An individual may transition between paid and unpaid work or underemployment, unemployment, temporary leave or retirement. And these factors don't suggest a lack of investment in paid work, or that they don't desperately want to be paid for the work that they do, or that they don't want to stretch or be challenged. In fact, the broader economic and societal environment shows that not only do people want to work when they are in periods of parenting or caring or looking after their mental health – in fact, it is good for people.

Which is all to say that there's an urgent need to gain more insight into how we can embrace this world of opportunity that we live in, and how we can also understand that, because of this new, exciting and dynamic environment, there are lots of other ways of engaging with work across the lifespan. Sustainability provides mutual benefit for the individual and the organisation, but more importantly, it provides an opportunity for the individual to have a career in the broader context of life.

CHAPTER 5

Seasons of Life

All the world's a stage,
And all the men and women merely players:
They have their exits and their entrances;
And one man in his time plays many parts,
His acts being seven ages.
– William Shakespeare, *As You Like It*

These words, written by Shakespeare for the character of Jaques in *As You Like It* just over 400 years ago, nicely capture a kind of intuitively appealing thinking familiar to us – breaking up big phenomena (like life) into smaller chunks so that we can better understand them. Clearly delineated and described stages, each with a sequence of physical and psychological phases, is a neat way of understanding life and our journey through it. It helps us to make sense of, and cope with, what is otherwise a complex set of dynamic experiences.

Newborns grow into babies, who become toddlers, who develop into early childhood, onwards to teenage years and later to adulthood. That journey has associated developmental milestones ranging from learning to walk and talk, to the emotional thunderstorms associated with becoming a teenager. I know I am looking forward to my now two-year-old leaving the developmental phase of the 'terrible twos', the one where cutting his morning toast in the wrong shape could bring a state of unreasonableness and anarchy. On the other hand, the impending teenage years and the emotional rollercoaster we are told lies ahead of us with our now tween (a new stage in which not yet teenagers begin to act like teens) girls – I am not sure how I feel about that.

The predictability of these phases of transition help us to understand the different needs we have as we travel through the seasons of life from childhood into adulthood and eventually, if we are lucky enough, to old age. Our education system, with yearly changes and transitions, signals movement based on chronological age. As we pass from class to class, or grade to grade, each year the shift is well mapped out, the switch from primary to secondary and onwards after secondary follows a relatively predictable ebb and flow, each with its own characteristic activities and roles. Based on this age and stage model we know, or at least we think we know, what should happen next.

The sequencing of life events, however, become increasingly nuanced as we grow into adulthood, as the change and transition associated with the academic calendar ceases to present the cues, 'What next?' becomes more like a set of vague clues, rather than a perfectly mapped-out path. This raises questions for us. What triggers movement from one phase to the next? Is it the start of each new year or decade of life, or is it a feeling? Does transition align with physical change and ability over time or has it to do with cognitive maturation? Do these stages overlap, occur in a predictable order, and during specific events? Is the process cyclical and enduring or full of stops and starts? How does this apply to your career, work and life, and what is the impact?

Careers and the seasons of life

Unsurprisingly, a social psychologist spotted this gap in our knowledge. Daniel Levinson, in a 1978 book entitled *The Seasons of a Man's Life*, postulated that, as adults, we also go through stable and transitional phases. His model outlines four main stages in our life structure: pre, early, middle and late adulthood. Using the metaphor of seasons to reflect the changes in life, Levinson wanted to assert the idea and build an understanding that no single phase of life is better or worse than any other, just different, each with its own unique challenges and beauty.

The parallels are clear: in the springtime (aligned with pre-adulthood) we plant the seeds for future growth; in the summer (early adulthood), through sunshine and just enough rain to avoid droughts, successful growth follows. In the autumn (middle adulthood) the fruits of a springtime of sowing and a summer of successful growth brings a bountiful harvest, while in the winter (late adulthood) growth slows and eventually brings death.

Based on Levinson's work, the notion of the stages of adulthood development found a way into the popular imagination. Central to this theory is the concept of 'the dream', or the desire to reconcile your life's ambitions with your career and work life. The desire to fulfil the dream is intensified in your late 30s, and for some brings turbulence. You are familiar with this idea: in your 30s, a time of transition, you make choices about family and career based on the decisions you made in your 20s. As you move out of your 30s you enter a BOOM phase (BOOM being short for Becoming One's Own Man!).

This BOOM is a phase of much conflict, according to this theory, as it heralds the onset of a personal crisis. Starting around age 40, he suggests, you begin to struggle with authority, yearn for more independence and, in many cases, question the choices your younger self made. During this phase, you may question the dream, and wonder, or worry, if you have made a lasting contribution in your personal and professional life. This often leads to a breaking-out phase (i.e. a mid-life crisis). A phase of this type can lead to change that is, for some, positive, and brings fulfilment; for others it leads to further pain and hardship. Once you hit your 60s, according to this theory, you are in a phase of decline, as you work your way towards retirement and death.

There are many appealing aspects of this theory, but it suffers from the same flaws as much of the rest of foundational psychology research in that Levinson undertook his research entirely on men. To be specific, his entire sample population consisted of 40 white, straight, cis-gender, college-educated, professional men living and working in America and aged in their 40s. In the 1980s Levinson conducted similar research with women, which was published posthumously, to explore if the same seasons could be applied to women's careers.[1]

He found that the same seasons of life were evident irrespective of gender; however, he acknowledged that some of the issues faced by women were different from those experienced by men. For example, he suggested that persistent sex and gender stereotyping tempered opportunities for women to access the paid workplace, thereby limiting opportunities for self-development.

He suggested that women struggled with 'the dream' due to the clash women experienced between their roles as both homemaker and career woman. He suggested women had a more complex dream than men, as work and career, though important, were less central to their dream. Levinson went on to argue that the findings in relation to women meant that the stages of life have universal applicability, but are manifested in different ways.

Since the publication of his works, other career theorists, including Donald Super, have used the age and stage model to develop a conceptual framework that supports our understanding of career and life development.[2] The arising WEIRD data we explored in detail in Chapter 2 led to the emergence of a rich field of critical thought around this age and stage model in contemporary vocational, career and work psychology. This field brilliantly challenges the assumptions underpinning age and stage models. Asking questions about the socialisation of people into the roles expected of them, and the arising sense of entitlement, or lack thereof, they feel to live life while having a career.

The seasons of life, but not as you know it

Considering careers as a series of ages and stages is, however, a useful framework, for several reasons. In the first instance, it provides a sense of predictability with some clues as to what you might expect all the while supplying language that helps us to communicate how we are feeling about those changes.

Secondly, neuroscience tells us that when you focus on small, singular tasks you allow your brain the opportunity to process information in bite-sized chunks first, which facilitates it to later make deeper connections between, within and across the data. This more streamlined cognitive process affords our brains the opportunity to collate all the data needed neatly and cohesively. As our brain is triggered to think about that one specific task, its ability to make connections between previously disparate pieces of information is greatly increased.

So, let's borrow from Levinson and think about shifts, changes and transitions, the ones that occur across the lifespan, to order our thinking and collate the data. But as we do let's view our seasons of change across a spectrum ranging from the sublime to the mundane, the brilliant to the utterly forgettable. Some of your seasons are strategic and the result of a well-executed strategy with aligned goals. Others just happened, such as the job offer you didn't expect or the promotion you didn't want or the pay rise. And, of course, there are those experiences that you would rather forget.

Together the good, the bad and the ugly combine to create a diverse and rich experience of life and career unfolding alongside each other. As we do it is important that we consciously detach (or, in the words of Gwyneth Paltrow and Chris Martin as they ended their marriage, 'consciously uncouple') our careers and lives from age, race, gender, sexual orientation or qualifications, and instead view them through the lens of human experience. As explored in earlier chapters these myths feed unsustainable careers rather than create the conditions to live life while making a living.

A human lens that not only respects but acknowledges that difference, at the most basic of levels, in all of its nuanced forms, is essential. Instilling diversity and belonging is important not because they are buzzwords, or because including a diverse workplace and ensuring workers experience a sense of belonging increases financial bottom lines, but because it is fundamentally the right thing to do.

It is possible to experience the various seasons in your story at the same time, or in non-sequential order. Lives are complex. Your unfolding career story may so far have only included some of the seasons. Across the course of your life, you may transition through some or all of the seasons. At times you may exist in a liminal space, a place between two or more seasons, and these are often moments replete with uncertainty. At times you may be unsure what season you are experiencing. And while some seasons are a choice, a decision that you exercise your agency over, and in which you feel a sense of control, others find their way quietly into your story, even if uninvited and unwelcome. Others announce themselves with an abrupt and unwelcomed bang, forming a central part of your story.

Coping at the edge of chaos

We each pass through the variety of these seasons in an unpredictable and non-linear fashion. The new world of work changes by the nanosecond. Something that didn't exist a moment ago now does, and another thing that did before, no longer exists, or has suddenly become redundant. In the twenty-first century, change is the new permanent. Learning to live and cope at the edge of chaos is a skill of survival.

For the most part, there is no way of determining what season comes next or a timeline for its arrival. This is an uncomfortable truth, perhaps, when all you want is certainty, and labels to attach to phases and stages.

Using this lens brings in from the margins the lived human experience of work and life, and this is essential to crafting a sustainable career. Integrating and weaving the seasons of life as an integral part of your story powerfully presents a counter-narrative, one that exposes the shortcomings in our workplaces and spaces where a corporate identity is assumed, one in which you are expected to work, deliver and remain productive no matter what is happening in other areas of your life.

Bringing those moments of change, the ones that impact *every* aspect of our life, into the story of our career is immense. Doing so invites life into our careers and grants permission to better understand how the different seasons of life impact our decision-making process. The collective power of sharing those experiences doesn't only force a tipping point that transforms your experience, it also blazes a trail for those who follow.

Autobiographical memory

Autobiographical memory is a complex skill unique to humans that allows us to defy our physical, temporal and spatial boundaries. Constructive and reconstructive in nature, our autobiographical memory helps us to recall, interpret and evaluate personally important interactions and experiences in our world. They form our internal monologue (the voice in your head), through which you self-define and make sense of who you have been and, more importantly, who you are yet to become.

Our capacity to create autobiographical memories allows us to shift perspective between the compilation of events that make up our lives. Our internal monologue considers how we have thought and felt about these events and informs how we might feel about them in the future. Using these memories, we author our personal internal history.

Interestingly, you are not born with autobiographical memory. Instead, you acquire it during your transition from late childhood into adolescence. As this learned, higher-order cognitive skill has been refined it has allowed you to connect with others, engage in conversation and find meaning in life.

Autobiographical memory in the context of your career speaks to your personal experiences of your work, life and careers as they intersect across time and contexts. The person who is the lynchpin of these memories, occupying the space in which each one connects, interconnects and diverges, is *you*. This makes understanding the unfolding seasons of life, and those that are yet to emerge, not only important in establishing a sustainable career but central to doing so.[3]

Blazing a trail through chaos

The concept of the seasons of life brought together in this way is novel. Firstly, it is based on what neuroscience tells us about how our brain likes to receive information as it makes decisions. Secondly, it emerges from practical, yet anecdotal evidence collected over the years while working with clients in individual and corporate settings. Beginning with thousands of pages of client notes, and considered reflection of those notes, finding a framework to support clients as they attempted to live life while having a career was important to their success. Based on this, the seasons of life metaphor strongly resonated, as it supplies the language to frame, express and reflect the experience of living and working in a new, more dynamic world. As such, this is not a theory evidenced in rigorous academic research; rather it puts language to theories that might otherwise not bridge the gap between science and practice.

From this perspective, the seven seasons – any one of which may apply to your life, your career or both – are as follows:

Liminality
Pause
Play
Progress
Survive
Explore
Reject

These seasons are not about affixing labels and putting feelings in a box. They are tools to aid self-reflection and therefore do not attempt to reveal perfect answers or structured solutions to complicated problems. Instead, they serve to support you as you creatively engage and craft a sustainable career, so that you can live life while making a living. Remember, your ambition is to find a sustainable way to flourish and progress in your life *and* career, now *and* in the future.

Underpinning each season are concepts that facilitate critical thinking and self-reflection. Together, they illuminate the importance of choosing the courage to be curious, a courage that leads to the cognitive flexibility essential in a future sustainable career, one where life and work operate in tandem during the changing seasons of life.

This framework and the language contained within it may feel unconventional, and it is, but it is also important to find a way to integrate it into your narrative if you wish to reset your relationship with your career.

Any of the seasons that you are about to read about may come before, after or within another. You may live through each season once, multiple times or in a variety of different sequences. The duration and depth of the season you find yourself in is likely to be different depending on other circumstances in your life at that time. This means that even if you enter and later re-enter the same season it is likely that your experience each time will be different.

Seasons of liminality

A season of liminality is characterised by change and transition, and is derived from the Latin word *limen* which literally means the space that exists between where you are now and where you are going as you transition across a threshold or boundary.[4] There are many times in life when you exist in a space somewhere between here and there, not quite knowing exactly where here or there actually is. This is the space that contains the knowledge of what was, and the known unknowns of what is to come.

For some the movement through a season of liminality is relatively easy and fluid as a new identity emerges. This positive experience encourages a form of productivity and creativity that brings about new structures and relationships in life. This sort of time-restricted liminality, one that oscillates from not yet knowing if *I am this or that*, to entering the space beyond the transition, where a new, more comfortable sense of *This is who I am (for now)*, brings a more positive outcome for the individual, and those they are connected to.

For others, the transition is much more complicated. In fact, there is research that suggests the progression through a season of liminality is often peppered with movement between free and easy to restrictive and hard, resulting in much more complicated experience.[5] This type of experience generates a sense that *I am neither this nor that* or perhaps *I am both this and that*. This experience of liminality can be negative in its impact as you exist in a heightened state of sensitivity as you try to determine what comes next.[6]

A season of liminality, the feeling of existing at the boundaries of two or more other seasons, can be driven by events in your personal or professional life. You may feel that you have a little, a lot of or no control over any or all of these experiences. The arising feelings and thoughts that drive your decision-making during a season of liminality can be flawed or fabulous, perfect or imperfect.

This can occur even where the transition is largely positive, expected and wanted. This is natural, as you are suspended in a most unusual way as you wait in anticipation for the next step, the future (your future) and what that may bring. The arising state of ambiguity and confusion happens during any change or process associated with transformation.

A liminal state is complicated by the interactions between you the person experiencing this liminal space, and your interaction with those around you, what they expect and want of you. It is also tempered by the associated societal, cultural, political and environmental expectations of what you should, or should not do or be. Often, it is the weight of these expectations that results in decision-making that does not reflect you or your needs or desires.

In the journey to reset your relationship with your career, and to find a sustainable career, one in which it is possible to thrive and progress in life and at work, both now and in the future, a season or multiple seasons of liminality should be expected. In fact, the two are inextricably linked as we change our relationship with our careers. This is particularly so if your identity and your career are so closely linked that you feel you cannot be who you are when you are not directly linked to your career.

Previously, we spoke of the challenges faced by mothers and carers who wish to return to the paid workplace after a period of unpaid work. This liminal experience has a massive impact on career progression among women who are mothers. There are, however, other less often spoken about forms of liminality. Brian O'Driscoll, spoke very publicly in a 2022 documentary called *After the Roar* spoke about the challenges of transitioning from elite professional sport into a so-called 'normal' life and career. Life-changing injury, trauma or sickness, in your life or the life of someone you love, that makes your chosen career path no longer a viable option, presents a season of liminality.[7]

Other research reveals the impact of this on men who work physically on-site in construction, who, as they age, become less physically strong. In that industry, youth and strength are privileged, and ageing men are often excluded from the jobs they once did with great pride and feel a sense of exclusion and uselessness, existing in the margins until retirement.

Seasons of pause

Seasons of pause are characterised by an acceptance, or realisation, that breathing space, the time to rest and recover, is essential. It is a recognition that moments of stillness are necessary for you to think deeply and consider – what next? You may choose to pause, or a season of pause may be forced upon you. Either way, you know, or come to realise, that during this season of life, the right way to grow into and develop a future sustainable career is to slow down or to stop altogether.

As you do this, you will likely continue in a job that supports your financial stability and independence, as you follow a different, slower pace of life. During a season of pause, your focus is to ensure that you have the time and space to do your job without any added stress or pressure. You do so in the hope that the arising cognitive freedom and psychological space provides you with the capacity to choose what you need to do in the present so that the path to a better future is paved.

In an always-on world, where a narrative of toxic positivity encourages you to keep going at all costs, the practical application of a season of pause can feel hard, if not impossible. This is to be expected.

You know exactly how hard it is to activate a season of pause in your career if, as you read this, you can think of job interviews you went to because you were expected to, not because you wanted to. Making the choice not to go forward, during this season of your life, would look like you weren't interested. But in truth you didn't want to go for the promotion, because life outside of work was so active in dictating your circumstances that putting yourself forward for that role would stretch your capacity beyond imagination.

This had nothing to do with the importance of your career, your dedication or ambition, rather it reflected a balanced decision to say 'not yet' – an incredibly thoughtful and responsible decision to pause in your career so that you could take care of life. But you swallowed your better judgement. You did this not because you wanted to, in fact you really didn't want to take it, but you knew that if you didn't you would be written off.

Frame it for yourself, understand it, but don't blame yourself. If as you reflect on your career, and in hindsight you know in your heart that there was that time you should have paused, please be kind to yourself. The myths of career choice and the broken world of work that we deconstructed in Part One operated silently in your decision-making framework, which denied you access to do what you needed during that season of life. A total reset with your career does not, and cannot, involve time travel to resolve decisions of the past. Instead, they serve as data points, pieces of information that guide you for the future.

Be kind to yourself. As you activate your Permission Mindset, allow yourself to explore this slower, perhaps more realistic pace of life as a possibility first, and then, if it is the right path for you, choose it consciously and own it as a practice.

Seasons of play

A season of play is characterised by a time of high energy and increased activity. Alert to what you want, you are open to opportunity. A season of play may involve taking a deep dive into your chosen career, new role or a different industry.

It involves making connections within and across your field. As you make these connections, you notice specific and attractive niche areas that particularly draw your interest. As your interest deepens, you look for opportunities, chances to build subject matter knowledge, flex your cognitive ability and gain transferable skills.

As you continue to play, you enter a heightened state of creativity that opens new vistas of opportunity to you. This heighted sense of creativity results in competency building, which in turn bolsters your courage to keep innovating in your role, industry or outside of your paid work. As this happens your confidence builds, and a positive cycle follows.

In a season of play, you do not choose work over life, or life over career; rather you have sufficient time and energy to invest in a meaningful life outside of work, while clearly feeling connected to paid work. In short, you are leading a full and meaningful life in your work, your life and your career. A season of play feels sweet; it is a time in your life when things are going well, and you feel that you are well positioned to enjoy it.

As you read that last sentence, make a note to yourself that this does not mean 100 per cent enjoyment, 100 per cent of the time. Achieving such heights of complete enjoyment is not the mark of a life well lived – complete or total existence, or the pressure to exist, at either ends of the spectrum of feelings and emotions cannot be sustained over time. It is only through knowing, and experiencing, the full range of the feelings that we can appreciate its opposite. Experiencing happiness is only possible if you know what it is to be unhappy. It is these very ebbs and flows, between the two ends of the spectrum, that make us human.

In a season of play, you feel physically and psychologically robust enough to comfortably cope with the full spectrum of emotions across time. You know that there will be ups and downs, but equally you are confident in your ability to cope.

Seasons of progress

A season of progress is characterised by a time of momentum in which you experience growth and development. In practice, this might present itself as a period during which you are gaining or developing the niche knowledge, skills, qualifications or abilities needed to advance in your chosen field, industry or career. Equally it could indicate a time during which you have decided to strategically invest time and financial resources in upskilling, reskilling or retraining in a bid to position yourself to do what you want in your next season.

Typically, a season of progress is a well-thought-out and strategically considered time in your life. As you engage with a season of progress you do so with a clear plan, with aligned and focused goals in place with which you are ready to engage, or have already engaged with.

To develop this clear and concise plan it is likely you have worked with a career development professional or coach to support you in your endeavour to make objective and well-considered decisions that lead to a sustainable career. As you work through this season an accountability buddy, someone you meet regularly to discuss your progression and to support you, plays a significant role in your life. An accountability buddy is someone you do not know well, but who you know well enough to ask for their support to objectively mentor you in a candid yet kind manner. You set the targets and decide on the outcomes, and your accountability buddy keeps you in line.

Since your ultimate goal is to flourish and progress in life *and* work during a season of progress, life outside of work is typically anchored and predictable, thus providing you with the space, time and energy to invest in career progression. This should not be mistaken as a suggestion that you should work all of the hours available to you, at the expense of your personal life and well-being. Or that the important people in your life should be accepting of taking a back seat while you focus on a season of progress in your career. If you have felt the need to stay late and to show interest even if that means missing an important life event so that you show ambition and commitment to your job and your career, you know the real price of progression at all costs. You have likely also asked yourself, 'Is this worth it?'

Seasons of survive

During a season of survive, you do whatever it takes to stay afloat. Characterised by chaos and a feeling of being overwhelmed, during this season you realise the need to re-evaluate, as you are uncertain about what comes next. In a season of survive, it is likely that your curiosity, courage, competency and confidence feel threatened.

A season of survive may be triggered by an unprecedented global event that changes the world on a macro level – for example when the dot.com bubble burst, or in the aftermath of 9/11, or during Covid-19, Brexit or the war in Ukraine. Such macro-level events have a global impact that is unpredictable and swift. Such events may lead to unexpected redundancy, redefined work patterns, unprecedented recessions or industry changes.

On a more micro, individual level, a health crisis, dealing with addiction, a relationship breakdown, getting fired or being promoted, a birth or a death may trigger a season of survive.

Attempting to embark on big changes or take on new challenges in your career may be a stretch too far. This might mean taking a step back or putting an exit strategy from your current role in place. It might also require you to enter a season of pause in your career, so that in the future you can move forward in both.

A word of warning during times of high intensity spurred on by a season of survival: you might be tempted to throw yourself into your work so that you don't have to deal with the personal impact of these events. Alternatively, you may decide to keep your true feelings to yourself, to protect others or to avoid facing your reality yourself.

While this may work in the short term, the pace at which you must sustain that level of engagement and output serves only to push the underlying feeling deeper down into the future. And withholding how you feel from important others in your life seldom works for anyone. This is not sustainable and does not prepare you to flourish and progress in life and in your career. It does not mean that you must tell everyone how you feel, but you can tell someone you trust.

After all, a problem shared is a problem halved. If you need to seek support from colleagues, family, friends or loved ones, or if you need help from professionals in other fields, give yourself permission to seek and receive that support.

As with all seasons, this season too shall pass, but as you move through it, do so with self-compassion and kindness.

Seasons of explore

A season of explore is characterised by curiosity. This is a time during which your senses and interests are heightened to contemplate and engage with new possibilities and potential different paths. You are hungry to learn more and to seek out change. During this season you are constantly researching, asking questions and talking to people both inside and outside your network to figure out what comes next.

It is an exciting time, full of questions for which you have few answers. This state of flux and uncertainty can feel exciting or overwhelming – perhaps even both at different times. How you feel about a season of explore often depends on your attitude to change, your ability to cope with that change and the type of support network you have around you.

During this near-constant state of wonder, as you experiment you are open to exploring novel opportunities that previously would never have crossed your mind. As you do so, you generate and test ideas as you attempt to refine developing notions about what to do next. As you do you might find yourself asking 'What if I did this or that?' or 'What if I could choose anything?' This experimental stance generates multiple possible avenues, some of which you are open to, others which you decide not to pursue further. Each possible avenue should lead to several possible iterations which you test and retest as you gain feedback.

Be careful in a season of explore as you can dally perpetually, ending up taking no action. While taking no action is

OK, it is only so if you are happy with what you have and your exploration was for fun, so to speak. If, however, you are serious about exploring, be clear about your 'why' and when you have enough data, advance with your plan.

Seasons of reject

During a season of reject, you decide (or the decision is made for you) to leave your job, role, industry, career or sector. In that moment, you are resolute that you are not going back to your old normal; instead you are choosing change. While this may be news to others, it is likely that change was something that occupied your inner thoughts for a very long time. The reality of your life as you were living it meant that seriously considering change was not for you in that moment.

This is a time to reject what you have done so far in favour of an entirely different professional future. While a season of reject is drastic it is not as all-encompassing as it might first seem. Absolutely, the task ahead is large, but you are not burning any bridges as you are still the same person, who continues to possess all the skills, experiences and learnings gained in and through the work you have done to date.

Although the career you are now rejecting is no longer what you do, most of the skills gained in that role are transferable. So while you might be starting afresh to learn the technical skills of the role, sector or career that your future self will work in, you are taking much more with you than when you started out on your career initially.

The vast majority, if not all, of your skills are transferable. Rather than starting completely afresh as if you are now a blank slate, you are this taking each of your skills, capacities, competencies and knowledge with you into the next season, and in whatever guise that takes you will use those for more success.

Armed with the knowledge that there are different seasons of life operational at different times, it is important to explore the seasons of your career so far, and to increase your awareness of their importance.

Some seasons see a focus on the unpaid work of parenting, on caring for and rearing others. During other seasons of life, you find that caring is directed towards yourself as you mind your mental well-being or recover from a health-related issue. You may have a time for travel, a time in which you explore the world, or move from one geographical location to the next.

Before your first Pause for 60 of this chapter, remember that, because your seasons of life are deeply connected to your identity, recalling them may trigger an unexpected emotional reaction. If this happens, be kind to yourself and take a break to recover. The tears, anger, disappointment or happiness are natural reactions, so activate your Permission Mindset and nudge yourself away from any self-directed harsh judgements.

Pause for 60 and the season of life (now)

Let's begin with a 10,000-foot view. Take your list of '&s', the ones that you committed to paper from Chapter 4. With a different-coloured pen, begin to explore the season you are currently in. This is the point at which you are going to connect data and information.

Interdependent careers

As you pass through and between these seasons you exist in a constant state of learning and discovery. Depending on the codes and rules that have driven your career so far, you may feel some, all or none of these feelings, as you learn to understand a sustainable career.

At times you will deeply feel your dependence on others as you try to sustain your career during particular seasons. Some of these people are close to you and offer support in the way that you need, while others are close and do not offer the support you want or need. The latter is harshly felt, whether expected or not. The sense that you and your needs are invisible or unimportant to, or misunderstood or misinterpreted by someone you love cuts deeply.

It can come as a shock when careers become linked, particularly during times of parenting or caring, when the sense of interdependence between you and significant others in your life perhaps for the first time impacts your career and the way you engage with your career. Start times, finish times, after-work drinks, impromptu evenings out (either together or with friends) – things that previously didn't involve the necessity to check in with someone else suddenly require a full tactical intervention. Everything is thrown up for negotiation, and it often takes a toll.

This interdependence may be re-contracted and re-negotiated as you and your partner, in caring or parenting, navigate this new reality. On the other hand, it may feel that only one person is doing all the re-contracting and re-negotiating, and that one-sided interdependence may feel unfair and unjust.

Loneliness, loss, grief and struggle often find their way to our door at times we least expect them, and present us with challenges and choices that are completely new to us. Harsh in their presence and all-consuming in the efforts they require of us, they often determine the next season of our career.

We don't have linear careers. We live careers in a way that is interconnected, living at the intersection of life and career. The more we normalise and talk about our career as a set of intersecting skills, built in and through work and life, the better.

CHAPTER 6

Tales of the Unexpected – Career Shocks and Catalysts

To expect the unexpected shows a thoroughly modern intellect.
– Oscar Wilde, *An Ideal Husband*

When Elon Musk, the new owner of Twitter, walked into its headquarters in October 2022 holding a kitchen sink, it was clear something out of the ordinary, perhaps even extraordinary, was about to happen. In the days that followed, the self-named Chief Twit (Elon himself) issued an ultimatum, via email, to Twitter employees. In that email he said that for them to 'succeed in an increasingly competitive world, we will need to be extremely hardcore. This will mean working long hours at high intensity. Only exceptional performance will constitute a pass grade.' The choice presented was simple: agree and stay (subtext: work at the expense of life), or click no and leave (subtext: no thanks, I am ready for a total reset). The resulting mass exodus of tweeps (the term people working at Twitter use to refer to themselves) has seen the company payroll shrink in size by over 3,000 staff. A wave of layoffs across technology followed, with Meta, Facebook's parent company, Microsoft, Netflix, Shopify, Stripe and other big players reducing their global workforce.

Technology, previously considered a 'safe' industry, was now less stable and more uncertain than previously thought. Highly qualified people, in roles that command significant pay, were, perhaps for the first time in their career, faced with the prospect of job loss. Those jobs were ended via email; thereafter, and with swift immediacy, their building and technology access ended.

Twitteresque corporate transformation Elon Musk style has the capacity (overnight) to wipe out whole teams, layers of management or parts of an organisation. The impact of such layoffs, at the behest of a business owner, can lead to turmoil for those involved.

Geopolitical upheaval like the war in Ukraine, or unprecedented global pandemics can have equally big impacts. There can be no comparison between war and tech industry layoffs in terms of their global impacts, yet these are both examples of instances where entire functions, roles, companies and associated careers are changed entirely or erased, meaning the best-laid career plans and advancement strategies sit entirely out of your control.

It is to these wrinkles in time, the personal and the wider societal ones, the ones that take your breath away, the stand-out moments that leave you wondering 'What just happened?', or even 'Did that *really* happen?', that we turn our attention. The inherently unexpected nature, or unexpected unfolding, of such events affects not only your career trajectory but also the season of life you find yourself in. These are your momentous moments.

What are momentous moments?

Likely you can recall events across the course of your life and career that brought welcome or unwelcome change. Collectively these events are called your momentous moments.

Momentous moments are defining moments, or moments that trigger change. Powerful in nature, these events stop you in your tracks, make you think and ultimately impact how you live, work and perform your career.

These are the big, audacious, stand-out events from life, work and career that you don't often think about but when you take a moment to reflect, they come flooding back, and in that moment, you realise their impact. These events are significant, and worthy of reflection. Not only do they have the capacity to shift your perspectives, to illuminate your thinking or change behaviour, often they change the course of your career and can trigger a change in the season of life.

So let's turn to consider yours – your unique collection of seemingly innocuous one-minute revelatory happenings in life. As with each of the other concepts we have explored and those we have yet to explore, this is not about uniformity. Your momentous moments, the ones that we explore here, are as unique to you as the individual fractals that combine to make a snowflake. Only you can name and define them. Personal or professional, outside of your control, or within your control, the important thing here is to engage with and acknowledge their existence. Even if the momentous moments that come flooding back are not what you expected, or don't seem that momentous, activate your Permission Mindset and allow yourself to let those experiences find their way onto paper.

Pause for 60

In your first Pause for 60 of this chapter, focus on the whole picture. Get the big events, stand-out achievements down on paper. Graduations, job changes, promotions, you know what they are. List them as they come to mind. Get each one down on paper and give it the space to breathe.

Once you have started the process, even beyond the Pause for 60, it is likely that you will continue to remember other momentous moments. Keep your notebook containing your list beside you as you continue to read, and as more of your defining moments come back to you, simply jot them down.

As you begin to think of your moments of change, be kind to yourself, and with your Permission Mindset activated, afford yourself the opportunity to own your moments of change and the role that you played in them.

Your list of momentous moments that sits before you contains the stand-out events across your entire life, encompassing the personal and professional. Likely, they are those you are proudest of, the achievements that make you smile, the times of excellence for which you feel incredibly proud.

Having these all in one place is magical, as it helps you to acknowledge what you have achieved to date, and the seasons of life through which you have travelled as you did so.

As we move from big-picture thinking to more granular considerations, you are going to Pause for 60 again, but with a different focus. This time you are adding detail and drawing connections.

Pause for 60

Add some more detail to your list. Take one or two of your most significant momentous moments and add more detail. Include the factors that may or may not have impacted your decision-making. Consider important people in your life, who contributed to those moments. What did you learn in and through those moments? As you get into the detail, ask yourself if there is anything that you would have changed about those momentous moments. Did each moment play out perfectly, or were there ups and downs? Where you can, add dates to your momentous moments.

As you sift through the data and delve into the detail of the information collected so far, you may begin to see connections between previously disparate dots. You may notice that there is a pattern emerging showing a cycle in your life. As you do this, cast your mind back to the seasons of life and ask yourself, during this momentous moment, what season of life was I in?

Remember, life and work are not separate, they coexist in the same space. So as you build the details of your career to date it is likely that your themes will start to emerge. It is also likely that these themes may not yet be apparent. Any reset involves time, so if patterns or themes don't make themselves known yet, don't worry. This is only the start.

One-dimensional is boring

Momentous moments run the risk of being one-dimensional and adding to the toxic positivity narrative. However, at the heart of this book lies the promise to help you reset your relationship with your career and support you to find a sustainable career, one in which you thrive, flourish and progress in life *and* work.

With that in mind, we need to turn our attention to extraordinary events that impact your career, that come in two different groups: first your career shocks; second your career catalysts. But first, a word of warning.

This transition can be jarring, so with your Permission Mindset activated, allow yourself to feel or think whatever it is that you are feeling or thinking. Denying yourself the opportunity to do this causes conflict between your body and brain. The ultra-speedy messengers sending messages from the control centres in your brain to those in your body go into a tailspin when this happens. When the messengers in your brain and body communicate with each other they like to be on the same page.

Imagine the messenger from your brain carrying to their team members in the rest of your body the simple message, 'I feel confused.' But when they arrive at their destination, they meet a closed door bearing a note reading 'Busy but not confused.' The messengers from your brain keep knocking, shouting the word 'Confused!' This goes on until the messengers are in conflict and you become stressed. This caricature replicates the disconnect between what your brain is telling your body and what your body is telling you when you decide to ignore, supress or just get on with things. Instead, if you acknowledge what you are feeling and what your brain is telling you, the messengers can spend their time on higher-order cognitive functions.

With that in mind, whatever you are feeling or thinking as you go through this chapter, pause, activate your Permission Mindset and allow yourself to align the message between your body and brain.

Career catalysts

Next, we are going to take a deep dive into your career catalysts.

Career catalysts are the major successes, triumphs or gains in your career to date. Referring to the big deals, events, decisions or ideas that retrospectively stand out across the course of your career, some common catalysts include an unexpected promotion, getting headhunted, a professional compliment from someone you admire, or a job offer arising from working on a personally meaningful project.

On a smaller scale, it might be the dedication you showed to honing a new skill or developing a professional area perceived as a challenge to your progression. For you it might be your attention to detail, ability to problem solve, capacity to innovate or subject matter knowledge that has amassed over time due to diligence, persistency and consistency.

Your career catalysts are the forces behind your career development to date.

Pause for 60

As you prepare to Pause for 60, activate your Permission Mindset, and with self-compassion allow yourself the opportunity to focus on your career catalysts.

Grab your paper and pens again, and at this stage get creative, using different colours and shades of pens or pencils. When you think about the idea of a career catalyst, a particular colour might come to mind, and if it does then write or highlight that specific catalyst in that colour.

Record your career catalysts, and as you do, attempt to align them, in rough chronological order, with your momentous moments. At this point you are gathering as much data as possible to help you connect dots, identify patterns and better understand your decision-making framework until this point.

> There are likely themes that each of our paths follow, although they may not come in the same chronological order that the rules tell us they will.

Resist the urge to uncouple yourself from your career catalysts and align them with luck. It's OK to own and acknowledge your role in your achievements to date. Most likely you had a team around you or people to support you in your endeavours, but it is equally likely that you played a specific role. It's OK to let yourself revel in your achievements every now and then.

If you need to go back and Pause for 60 again, do so. Collating this information is vitally important. There are enough people in the world to tell you what you do wrong or could do more of – you don't need to start doing it to yourself. As you take a further Pause for 60, you are unsure of how to start, use the following questions to guide you.

Pause for 60

As you think about your career catalysts, focus with candid clarity on the specific role you played in each of them. So often, we offer up our work and accomplishments as being due to a great team. If that is the case, stop, and as you do, activate your Permission Mindset and focus on the following quesitons:

- Were you part of a team or did you work as an individual?
- What was your unique contribution?
- Write it down, record it, and then own it.

Career catalysts are hard won, and the story that accompanies them is often one of luck.

- Was I in the right place at the right time?
- I had a great team and without them would it never have happened?

Sound familiar?

As you think about your career catalysts, go with your gut; include what feels right for you. There is no right or wrong way to spend your Pause for 60, there is only your way.

Once your Pause for 60 ends, drop your pen and sit back.

Naturally, if you feel like continuing, do just that. Remember, your aim is to get words, doodles or bullet points down, it's not to create a beautiful piece of prose. The function of the data you are collecting is to provide the raw information upon which you craft the story of your sustainable career.

Here are some of my career catalysts:

- Gained admission to university 1998
- My postgraduate graduation from Trinity College in 2005
- Organising and facilitating a careers exhibition for rural children 2007, 2009
- Asking that 'question' at the IMAGE event 2014
- Setting up my own business 2015
- Sitting on the Google Compass panel in Google Ireland HQ 2018
- Securing a place on ACORNS, a support for female-led rural businesses 2016
- Securing my first retainer with a large organisation 2019
- Beginning study at University of London 2019
- First appearing on national radio and television 2017
- HarperCollins*Ireland* approach to write this book 2021
- Finalising the copy of this book 2022

You may find this task challenging, and you may feel you have no or only a few career catalysts. Or maybe, each time you think of one, your inner critic speaks up and presents a reason not to include that item. If this is the case, you are not alone, and it is for that reason that we created the Permission Mindset.

It is also important to remember that this is an exercise in quality rather than quantity. It doesn't matter if you have one or multiple career catalysts to record; it is about the meaning of those specific moments to you in your career and their impact on your overall career development.

What are career shocks?

A career shock is a disruptive and extraordinary event, caused by factors outside of your control, that triggers a deliberate thought process in relation to your career. Career shocks shake you to the core, often coming from nowhere, or as a slow crescendo. While the long-term outcome of a career shock may be positive or negative, career shocks in the moment of experience have the capacity to significantly influence how and why you make decisions about your career. So profound are these shocks that often they serve as the trigger for a change in the season of life. In short, career shocks are not for the faint-hearted but they are the lived experience of professionals the world over.

Equally, career shocks are those awful moments that nobody expects will happen to them. These are the negative events that undermine your confidence, reduce your employability and impact your decision-making. The scale and frequency of career shocks are dependent on a myriad of factors.

Some major career shocks are both disruptive and extraordinary, and you typically have no agency over their impact on you. Examples could include redundancy due to Covid-19 or the financial recession in 2010. These types of career shocks are relatively easily explained, as the majority of the workforce were impacted by this same shock.

On the other hand, at a time of high employment, being fired, made redundant or replaced by a more junior staff member may take a little more explaining to yourself and to others. If you have experienced workplace bullying or incivility at work, or worked in a toxic environment, despite your lack of control over your circumstances, the career shock is real.[1]

My personal story

My career shock threatened to upturn the story of my career path altogether, and at one of the most vulnerable and joyous times in my life, just after having my first baby. In fact, it stripped me of my identity.

Prior to going on maternity leave, I was headfirst in my career. It consumed me, and I had all the time in the world to commit to it. I could start early and pick up the pieces late at night if I needed to, while still managing to do all of the fun stuff outside of work. But shortly after having my first baby I was told the job I had left no longer existed, and that I would have to return to a new job, one that I had no training for and no experience in.

I was devastated.

I had fundamentally believed that something like this only happened to other people in different careers or different organisations. This unrequested, unwanted and unnecessary career shock tore me apart. And, if I am honest, some 10 years later I still struggle with the impact. I did not, and still cannot, understand how my transition to motherhood altered the perception of me or my ability to do my work. Neither can I understand how an organisation could act in such a way.

During that time I occupied a season of liminality, a place of great uncertainty, an in-between area that exists between person, professional and parent. Research shows that this liminality, a time of transition, is a normal, yet seldom spoken about, space for new mothers to occupy as they transition between old and new identities. For the remainder of my maternity leave, my season of liminality as a new mother became extended into my professional life, where I entered a limbo land in my career.

I did not return to my old job after my first or even my second baby. I didn't have the opportunity to. I never got to say goodbye to my colleagues or got the chance to talk about my new business. I had no control or agency, and my voice which once afforded me the position to advocate for others failed me when I needed it for myself. The professional journey that followed was heart-breaking, and I ultimately left a job I loved and colleagues I adored.

From the outside, it looked like I had made the choice to leave and not come back, but the reality was very different. I struggled. Yes, I always dreamed of running my own business, but it was never my intention to set up a business after mothering two small babies. This was a time when we as a family needed a season of pause, one in which the stable and secure income that my job provided us with would offer stability. Initially, when I started to work in my new business, I worked for free. I wrote articles, spoke at events, delivered training for exposure. For the first three years in business, it cost me money to go to work.

Some years later, while speaking at an event for International Women's Day, I was asked by a fellow panelist, who was a prospective client, about my previous work. I had prepared for this, and I could offer a story, but she was focused in her curiosity. As the conversation deepened, she asked me a straightforward, simple question: 'Did any clients follow you from your old organisation when you set up your own business?'

I froze, my throat closed and my hands began to sweat. I am sure she could see the fear in my face. I had no story to tell, and, in that moment, I could find no words to explain what had happened. In that moment I revisited my season of liminality, trying to come up with an answer, I felt visible and invisible.

Pause for 60.

As you get your pen and paper begin to record your Career Shocks. Go into as much detail as you feel comfortable with and outline what your Career Shock looked, or looks like. What season of life were you in when you experienced your career shock? As you write, activate your Permission Mindset and be kind to yourself. This is not easy but it is helpful.

Career shocks and unusual outcomes

'Making the best out of a bad situation' and 'What's for you won't pass you' are both phrases that I heard at least once during my career shock.

While the ultimate outcome was not all bad, it remains a part of my career narrative that I am grossly uncomfortable with, and it produced a gap in my career that is hard to explain, particularly as it coincided with the exact time in my life when I was 'expected' to opt out of paid work to engage with my responsibilities as a mother. This expected opting out was a choice I never wanted to make but I was somehow forced into it. The hugely emotional reaction I had was dubbed as post-natal depression, which I did not have. When I sought out and got the support that I needed from a qualified mental health professional, she was able to differentiate between Post Natal Depression and the anxiety I was experiencing. My personal identity, like those of many others, is (and was then) so closely linked to my career that I struggled in that season of life. The career shock of being told that upon my return from maternity leave I would have to do a job that I was unqualified for was the catalyst.

It is only recently that I can speak about this season of life without an overt emotional reaction. So to suggest that our careers and our lives are not intertwined is ludicrous. The stories intersect and they impact each other.

To learn to acknowledge the impact of career shocks with both compassion and kindness is an act of bravery. It is the start of a new narrative that informs the structures and leadership of our current and future workplaces, one that it is essential for ensuring that your future career is one in which you thrive, flourish and progress in life *and* at work. It is also incumbent upon organisations and organisational leaders to ensure that the opportunity to thrive, flourish and progress is open to all.

Liam's story

As you can see, career shocks come in all shapes and sizes. A career shock may also be of your own making. Take the example of Liam, who wanted to lead a project at work to gain a stretch opportunity, despite several mitigating factors that clearly showed that other colleagues, including a close friend, were better suited to this project. Liam pushed hard to get this role and lead the team, even resorting to calling in personal favours. In doing so, he was clear in the knowledge that he would likely cause upset within the team, and with at least two of his colleagues, which would result in a negative ripple effect in an otherwise good team morale.

Throughout the project, he struggled to lead the team, to show relevant subject matter knowledge and to build collaboration. Liam had never had these issues previously. Undoubtedly, poor leadership was shown by those who made the decision to put Liam in the role. However, it must not go unnoticed that Liam exercised his agency and leveraged relationships to secure a role that he should not have otherwise been allowed to take on. At performance review time,

Liam got his lowest ever career review. Not only did he fail to get a raise, he was also put on a six-month performance management review. He was devastated, not to mention feeling isolated, since his colleagues no longer trusted him.

Liam had faced career shocks before, having been made redundant in his early career, but this felt different. He hadn't been alone in his redundancy; he had been one of 300 who were let go. Conversely, Liam knew he had directly contributed to this career shock, and it was his to take on his own. He had agency, and in exercising it he had caused strife for others and placed himself in a professional quandary, and all of this impacted his life both inside and outside work.

Over the six months that followed, Liam met performance management targets and managed to heal relationships, but ultimately he left the organisation. On reflection, he understands that his desire to fast-track his route to leadership through a role that he forced his way into meant that he brought about a self-inflicted career shock.

Did he learn from it? Absolutely. Would he do things differently next time? One hundred per cent. The impact had been harsh, ultimately derailing his career and shaking his confidence. When curating his career story, Liam did not want to talk about this career shock. In fact, he didn't reveal it until late in our time working together. He was embarrassed and ashamed. Over time, he realised that including it in his personal career story but choosing not to share it with colleagues or employers allowed him to retain ownership. He did this while ensuring that through self-reflection he learned the importance of respect for others and their skill sets while retaining his strong career ambitions.

Coping with career shocks

There is no doubt that career shocks are hard to come to terms with, and they do significantly impact your decision-making process. They are often written off the page to serve as background information or, more often, kept hidden. Despite the impact of these emotional responses, these shocks are important. Sharing them with others or integrating them into your story is a personal choice that is dependent on context. But understanding them and weaving them into your understanding puts you in a position of agency and control over your story. Based on that understanding, you can share as much or as little as you feel comfortable with. What is vitally important about that understanding is that you use it to inform your future decision-making.

Personally, when I undergo this process, I find my career shocks emotional to write down, hard to think about and even harder to talk about. In fact, so emotionally triggering are my career shocks that, for many years, I spoke to no one about them, not even the people I loved and trusted the most. I held them close, said nothing and continued as if everything was OK. Moreover, I blamed myself for them, believing even that I had done something to deserve them.

Even now I find it hard not to engage my harshest inner critic, who with candid criticism scolds me. When I did this exercise as part of a course, such was the trigger of recalling the eight or so years that I was in a particularly toxic role that I had to request an extension in submitting the written reflection.

As you read what follows you may judge my character and imagine a weak, emotional and protected woman, unable to cope. If you do, I don't blame you. I levelled that exact criticism at myself. Yes, I am a well-educated, able woman who grew up in a position of relative privilege. While my family are not wealthy, we never wanted for anything. I lived in a home full of love and shared evenings and weekends with extended family and friends.

But in my first role out of college I was terrorised, and I struggled to cope. I didn't think anyone would believe me if I told them what was happening, and I fundamentally believed that I deserved it. I spoke to others to temperature-check my situation, but using the 'a friend of mine' third person narrative to conceal the reality of my work life. I was met with uniform responses of shock and astonishment that someone would be subjected to such corrosive behaviour. The advice given to my 'friend' by these confidantes could be summed up as follows: 'Tell her to get out, she needs to leave before it's too late.' However, this was often followed with something like: 'Clearly, she must go, but if she wants to work in this country again, tell her to move on and say nothing, because if she tells what is happening to her, her career is over.'[2]

I thought the same, so I tried to manage shock after shock. I know now that I had not been alone in facing this sort of conundrum, and if you experience workplace incivility, bullying, abuse or harassment, you are not alone either. These toxic behaviours are in most workplaces in some shape or form, and they have crippling effects not just on the victim, but on the organisation as a whole. And it is not just the individual receiving the ill treatment who suffers. For witnesses to this behaviour, even if not directly impacted, over time the toxicity takes a toll, impacting their ability to engage with their work and deteriorating overall feelings of well-being.

Sexual harassment in the workplace

Despite the human toll and the impact on business outcomes, we remain really poor at adequately addressing these issues. A national survey of Irish workers found that 56 per cent of bullied employees discussed the matter with their employer, but only 23 per cent took the problem further to HR. Why is the rate of workplace bullying so high, but report rates shockingly low? The most straightforward answer is fear: fear of humiliation, fear of losing your job, fear of not being believed, fear of being isolated, fear of being labelled a troublemaker.

That fear is tangible and visceral, especially when accompanied by shame.

For me, the easiest way to cope was to say nothing, swallow my feelings, work really hard and put on my poker face. I'm not sure if you have a poker face, but when growing up we would activate it when playing competitive sport. A poker face is the exact opposite of the explosion of emotions John McEnroe was renowned for on the tennis pitch. Instead of letting the rage and frustration out and showing weakness to your opponent, you showed no emotion in your words, face or body, no matter what was happening. Wearing a poker face is a familiar experience for many who have suffered incivility and toxicity in the workplace.

For many women, and young women in particular, trying to advance in male-dominated sectors, sexual harassment is a very real and dark reality. Sexual harassment often takes the form of the suggestion (or demand) of a quid pro quo – an exchange of sexual favours in return for a benefit or promotion. The resulting power imbalance often results in a hostile work environment for the more junior person. A shocking report by the US Equal Employment Opportunity Commission in 2020 found that 55 per cent of victims experienced retaliation in the workplace after reporting sexual harassment. These punishments ranged from demotions, to job loss, to exclusion from staff activities.[3] We need only to consider the treatment of women who speak out against such harassment. Labelled as taking things too seriously, or being overly sensitive, their experience is often minimised, and the default position is to doubt and disbelieve her, and to question what she did to contribute to the experience.

The #MeToo movement drew global attention to this, and highlighted the gender power imbalance within the workplace that underpins sexual harassment, bullying and harassment against women at work. Equally, the media, through TV programmes such as *Maid* on Netflix and *Liar* on BBC, demonstrates the inadequacies of legal systems in supporting abused women. These harrowing shows highlight the punishment that women who complain face, and the battles they have to go through to be seen and supported. While #MeToo empowered women to speak out, we still have a long way to go.

Keeping this in mind, begin to consider your career shocks. While you may not have directly experienced a toxic workplace, incivility or harassment, there are other shocks that you may have experienced. Remember, just as with career catalysts, your career shocks are as unique to you as your fingerprints.[4]

Unexpected career shocks

A client I worked with included the birth of his children as a career shock. He realised that he was expected to trade time with his children to intensify work patterns, and he really didn't want to do that. His own father had been absent through most of his childhood, and before he passed away he spoke of the great regret he experienced not spending time with his young children. The Happiness Study by Harvard, the longest-running study on human behaviour across the lifespan, empirically backs up what his father felt, finding that the greatest regret of life was spending too much time at work and not enough time with family.[5]

Acknowledging this career shock brought my client to the realisation that he was going to do things differently. Based on this, together we crafted an 18-month career exit strategy from his current role and built a sustainable career development plan. Three years later, he and his family have moved closer to his partner's family, and he works in the same industry with a fully remote organisation. Although he compromised on his pay, they are better off now, as they have a smaller mortgage. After the move, his partner returned to the paid workforce. Many factors impacted this. The availability of her family to support with childcare, access to more affordable childcare, and the ability to now share pick-up's and drop-offs all contributed.

Career shocks come in all shapes and sizes. Refusing to acknowledge them leads only to more of the same thinking, which brings more of the same doing. As you sit in front of a page full of sentences, doodles or random words, it might at first seem hard to find a connection between your moments of change, your career boosts and your career shocks.

Pause for 60

As you begin your next Pause for 60 you may feel that your insights are linked but not yet a story. Your insights are linked but they are not yet a story. The connections are covert, and the subtle way the dots connect are as yet unclear. A little something magical happens next. Take your time, and as you begin to look for and identify connections between dates, times, decisions and events, slowly things will begin to align and cohere. Most likely, previously missed connections become apparent, or you realise the impact of that moment of change on the rest of your career.

The old adage 'hindsight is 20/20' comes to mind. The first time I did this exercise (and this is mirrored with clients constantly), it was insightful and frightening, not to mention emotional. The process of sitting down and physically putting it all on paper revealed to me the impact that having my children had on my career. The birth of our first daughter meant that for the first time my career choices were deeply connected to and interdependent on someone else. The decisions I made, the manner in which I chose to engage with my work, what I said yes to and what I said no to – all of this now really mattered. While it had always mattered, the weight of that yes or no used to lay on my shoulders alone.

If I chose to do something, I could work (or not) to get it completed. But now it was no longer about the impact of those choices solely on me; now it meant that I had to consider the impact of those choices on her.

The liminality of my existence, the in-between space that I occupied, was so new to me that it scared and excited me all at once. There is an Irish phrase, *ar bís*, that nicely captures that liminal space – the feeling, or a state, that sits between nervousness and excitement, an inbetween feeling of not knowing what is to come, unsure of what has gone before and a feeling of suspense as you wait for what comes next.

Fiona's story

Fiona, after a whirlwind romance, married Joe, and together they entered postgraduate studies. Joe and Fiona were both part-time students, however Joe was working full-time, and Fiona was full-time guardian for her two younger siblings.

In her 20s, Fiona's life circumstances dictated her career choices. Her father died when she was a young child, and just as she was about to start college, her mother became terminally ill with cancer. Fiona had two younger siblings in secondary school at the time, and somehow, she managed to graduate while caring for her mother and siblings. After graduating, she didn't have the privilege of choosing a career; she had to work to support her siblings. Choosing a job close to home was a priority. Proximity to home afforded her the opportunity to earn money, which allowed her siblings to remain in education. It also meant that she could care for her mother. She made this choice not because it was what she had trained for, or because it was what she wanted to do, but because she needed to work. When her mother died, Fiona, now an adult orphan and the primary carer for her siblings, continued in that job.

Now in her mid-30s, she works in an area she loves. Her siblings are older now and less dependent on her. She secured a place on a graduate training programme in a large global multinational to train as an accountant and remains in a long-term relationship with her life partner.

They want children, but Fiona fears that pregnancy and motherhood would scupper her chance to build a career in her industry. If she chose to have children now, then returning to the paid workplace in her late 30s, perhaps early 40s, with small children, and no paid work experience, she fears, would be an insurmountable challenge. If, however, she establishes herself now, she thinks that maybe in five years she could have children without such a big professional impact.

Children as career shocks

Ar bís is, in other words, nervous excitement. I knew what it meant from my wonderful Irish teacher Ms McEnroe Lynch, but I had never felt it viscerally. Not, that is, until the morning after our first daughter was born. On 4 February 2012, I sat in bed holding her. I had given birth by caesarean section, which meant I could hold her but not lift her until the doctors made their rounds that morning. Sitting in my room, alone, on a bright February morning, I felt *ar bís* – I wasn't quite sure how to be a mother, let alone a good mother.

Yes, I had an amazing role model in my own mother, but this was me, just me, becoming a mother. I was terrified – terrified of breaking her, both emotionally and physically. I was overwhelmed, scared and excited. Sitting on that bed, getting to know my baby, I made her a promise, a maternal promise that mothers all over the world whisper. The words were as simple as they were heartfelt. I said, 'Saibhe, I promise to love you unconditionally, to teach you right from wrong, and to be your role model.'

Combined, these words took the form of my first promise to her, and I was resolute to keep it. Six weeks later, I did just that. I said no for the first time in a very long time. Faced with two paths, in the immortal words of Robert Frost, I had taken 'the one less travelled by. And that has made all the difference.' But I also paid a price. What followed was a truly awful chapter in my career. And for my daughter, coming into a world and watching her mother deeply unhappy in her work due to workplace bullying and discrimination was not the role model she deserved.

So I said 'No', and it formed a complete sentence, bringing about massive change in my life. I lost my job as a result, but I successfully brought the discrimination case through the legal system. Something else also changed though – something within me. I made that same promise on the day after each of my other three children were born. It has not been an easy promise to keep, but that decision changed fundamentally the story of my career, my partner's career and the future career stories of our children.

As they grew from babies into the children they now are, they saw a couple fight for what is right, even when it was the hardest thing to do. They now watch me go to work with a smile and come home with that same smile, nearly all the time. When I work late evenings or early mornings, they see a mother going to work because she wants to and enjoys it. She doesn't make a choice between work and home; rather, in and through her the story of work, life and career unfolds.

As I write this book, the story of my career is one I am proud of. While I would not have chosen some of the events, they have changed me and my family. Each day I go to work my choice is to positively impact the structure and culture in workplaces so that women who are mothers feel entitled to a career. Where organisations fail to ensure that entitlement exists, it is my ambition to ensure that those women find an organisation that recognises their excellence and brilliance, not *despite* being a mother but *because* they are a mother.

And since a rising tide lifts all boats, the impact of workplaces becoming more inclusive of working mothers, of addressing workplace structures that are either implicitly or explicitly exclusionary, means that other under-represented groups in the workplace can benefit from such changes. That's not to mention the more permissive conversations that our workplaces need to have about how men who are fathers are entitled to perform that role. As men transition into fatherhood, this often coincides directly with a period of work intensification. So while women who are mothers engage with mothering, men who are fathers do not feel entitled to engage with fathering. Fathers' construction as the primary breadwinner places, almost exclusively, the emotional toll of earning a wage to put a roof over his family and food on the table as a core responsibility of his socially and culturally accepted role; all at the expense of time with his family.

Pause for 60

With pen in hand and your Permission Mindset activated, try to list your career shocks, should you have them. At this point, you may or may not have the words to fully describe your career shocks or their impact, but this is not a race towards perfection. As you hone in on your career shocks, align them with your momentous moments. No doubt this is challenging and if you are emotionally triggered by this Pause for 60 then stop. This may be a sign that you need professional support to cope with the events of your career shock. If not, as you match your career shocks to your momentous moments, consider if your shocks shifted your season of life. As you end this Pause for 60 take a break and do something kind for yourself.

Positive or negative – catalysts and shocks

Intuitively, we align career catalysts with positive outcomes and career shocks with negative outcomes. The unique thing, however, about momentous moments, career shocks and career catalysts, is what happens in the aftermath. Catalysts do not always align with positive outcomes, and shocks are not always equated with negativity. In fact, some career catalysts reveal themselves, over time, as negative, while some career shocks, again over time, have a net positive effect. The only way to understand the impact, effect and outcome of both career shocks and career catalysts is to understand them.

By taking a deep dive into the dynamic and interconnected experiences that you have lived, what you have learned from those experiences, what you have gained and what you would change, you develop an understanding of what you want, why you want it and how to get it. Let there be no doubt, doing this is far from a simple challenge, but it is equally a game changer when it comes to understanding how your career has developed over time.

Pause for 60

At this point, Pause for 60. In your 60 seconds of reflection, focus on the impact of your moments of change, career shocks and career catalysts. As you do, remind yourself that it is possible that your career shocks brought about positive outcomes and your career catalysts brought about negative outcomes. Consider how the story of your moments of change, career shocks and career catalysts combined help you to understand what got you to where you are now.

As the picture builds, use this outline information to develop a deeper comprehension of how you made decisions about life, work and career during the various seasons of life. Remember, these events are not separate; together, they combine to facilitate your understanding of what got you to now.

All the while, we must remember that there may be points in your life when your career story is about choosing financial stability over enjoyment. At other points it may be about coasting in a job you could do with your eyes closed, so that you can engage fully with a busy life outside of work. At still other times it may be about stepping out, up or sideways, depending on your identities outside of your working life, but in the understanding that your story during this season of life positions you in a space of relative agency.

When we engage with a story, our mind's eye is captured, and we embark on a creative journey, through which small clues about characters created through words, spoken or written, come to life. We each fill in the blanks about who, what, when and where. We create images that develop into ideas, and when we stop, the story lives on. As we go about our daily business, our spatial and temporal realities collapse and our mind wanders back and forth to the pages, the words and the story. Guided by the writer, we each experience the world through a different lens. These stories remind us that, while our body is locked into the certainty of the here and now, we can perform creative somersaults in our imagination, as we travel through space and time.

Takeaways

While the story of my personal and career moments of change at first seem disconnected, when they are placed in the same space, connecting the dots between what happened then and what I do now is a sense-making process. It does not mean that I (or you) have to reveal with complete vulnerability the nuances of that season of my life, nor does it require that I relive the pain associated with that chapter. Nor does it require denial – denial of the pain, the joy or the harshness of that period. What's more, taking that deep dive revealed a tenacity that I never knew I possessed, a skill that I proudly take with me time and again.

Of course, the requirement for Pollyanna positivity and the belief that from all bad things come good should be mitigated here. I would *never* have chosen this story, and if I could time travel and erase certain aspects, I 100 per cent would. The deep hurt brought about by certain moments, the deafening silence of colleagues afraid to speak up for fear of their own job, the shame and embarrassment of speaking out for fear that I wouldn't be believed, and the fear that I had done something wrong were absolute.

Did I learn from this chapter? Yes, absolutely. I learned that using numbers and data to convert a job into an object robs the role of its soul and humanity. It dehumanises the person and it steals the heart of an organisation. I learned that where kindness and compassion are present, and they drive organisational values, this would never happen to a woman returning to work after maternity leave.

Would I choose to experience this again for the value of that learning? No way, never in a million years. Will I use the negative to bring about good? Yes, but it still hurts like hell. This part of my career story is one from which I will never fully recover. Yet learning to craft it as a chapter of my career story means that I can cope with it. Understanding it in this way does not mean that it must be revealed to all. There is a time and a place for everything. In fact, there was a time that doing so would have been foolish, and most likely would have resulted in negative outcomes both personally and professionally.

Instead, learning to craft the story and allowing it to emerge at points of intersection between your career and personal moments of change places you in a position of agency and power over the details of that narrative. In so doing, it connects the personal to the professional and affords you the opportunity to understand your story and, to use it to build your sustainable career from the lessons learned.

Your story may be different from mine, but if you have taken time off to be a mother or a carer, that 'gap' in your paid employment is often one that glares from your CV, serving to hold you back from applying for that job, going back into paid employment or taking the next step in your career. Choosing to acknowledge that gap, own it and weave it into the very heart of your career story brings a level of courage that cannot be overestimated. Remember, as you do unpaid work, you are building skills that are relevant to the workplace – valuable skills that are readily transferable.

CHAPTER 7

Your Career, Raw and Unfiltered

When I was in New York City during the summer of 2001, I bumped into Julia Roberts in Saks Fifth Avenue. She was shopping while I was essentially just sightseeing, afraid to even touch the clothes, single items of which cost the equivalent of a month's rent. I recognised her immediately, as she looked exactly like the woman I knew from *Pretty Woman*.

Years later, pre-Covid, I was speaking at an event, and the headline speaker was an influencer I follow on Instagram, who shall remain unnamed. When I was introduced to them, I had no idea who they were. They looked nothing like the curated version of themselves online. They looked great, mind you, but still totally different. Filters online rendered them unrecognisable in real life.

Filters are the modern-day equivalent of dress-up. Initially a fun gimmick, filters allowed you to add glasses or a moustache, morph into an alien or become a puppy dog complete with ears and a cute pink nose. Now they allow you to 'beautify' your appearance by changing your face to look like a better, or different, version of the 'real' you. You can erase, sharpen, enhance, shrink, recolour, or remove the parts of you that you don't like.

It should come as no surprise, then, that using this very

specific form of augmented reality to enhance, change or distort how you look is big business. In fact, the most widespread use of augmented reality isn't in business or gaming but in the world of social media beauty. The associated beauty standards, the curated aesthetic and the portrayal of perfection through the lens of filters has brought about the phenomenon of the digital self. The most successful influencers have curated their 'perfect' image, even if it looks totally unlike the 'real' version.

Have you ever taken a selfie and played around with filters that alter your image – even for fun? I have, for both business and pleasure. But no matter what angle I use, or at what distance I hold my phone, I always notice something about my face that I don't like, something 'wrong' with me. Even the selfies I take with my kids, I try to catch only a slice of my face, so that I get all of them, so that while I am technically in the picture, I am but a sideshow. I try all the tricks, hacks and ideas from influencers, but none of them work, ever.

You might wonder, and rightly, what do influencers, filters and a selfie have to do with you or your career? Well, bear with me. If a selfie is an enhanced version of you, arrived at using modern technology to help you appear different and, perhaps some might argue, better than the real you, then it isn't the greatest stretch to suggest that the story of your career, the one you present to the world, may in fact be filtered and different to your real, unfiltered, internal career story.

Unfiltered careers

Maybe the filtered version of your career looks 'perfect' from the outside but, deep down, you know that the image of perfection is unsustainable, and you are struggling. Perhaps you never liked your career, where you work or the industry you trained in. Maybe you started out loving it, but as you progressed up the ladder, your career and the things that you love about it are no longer part of your role. It could be that the only way to progress in your career was to leave the parts you love behind, so that's what you did and, well, now you regret it. You may have inherited your career from your family and feel like you never had a choice. You may have been told what to do, and to keep the peace you did just that. Perhaps you had invested in a particular career path, studied for years, and now work within the field, so now that you have made your choice – that's the end of the story.

You may have reached a hierarchical position in your organisation or your role beyond, which makes opportunities for progression or development difficult, and while you are busy, you are not challenged; in fact you are bored. This is a very particular feeling, and in organisational psychology we call it 'rustout'.[1] Rustout is related to burnout, and in fact presents with the same symptoms; however, the root cause is not overwork, it is boredom, lack of challenge and a feeling of staleness. On the other hand, you may feel indifferent, neither loving nor hating your career, just going through the motions to get to retirement.[2]

These sorts of career experiences happen to most of us at one time or another, but most often they pass after a period of time. For others, however, they linger and impact each other aspect of life. There is no right or wrong way to handle these feelings, as they differ from person to person. You may be the kind of person who chooses to tell everyone how much you hate your job and want to change your career. Or you might be the kind of person who quietly gets on with things, finding it easier to say nothing, while in the back of your mind you feel stuck.

Based on experience, I suggest that the best approach to take when addressing these sorts of issues is slow and steady wins the race. The reason is basic: when you give yourself the space and time to process information, you allow yourself the opportunity to make connections that you previously didn't see. You may still make these connections if you go faster, but slowing down provides the bandwidth you need to go a little deeper.

If you do choose to go at your own, swifter, pace, ensure that you activate your Permission Mindset. Also, promise that if you find that this swifter pace doesn't work for you, you will reconsider your decision.

Pause for 60

In this Pause for 60, focus on slowing down. As you enter into this chapter, activate your Permission Mindset and give yourself permission to slow down (even a little bit). Remember, this is giving yourself permission to think about things from a new perspective, through an unfiltered lens. Remind yourself this is not uncharted territory; you already know what you are thinking. Orient yourself to take this snapshot in time, a Career Selfie, from which you gain insight and understanding into your career so far.

This is your time to recall the details of your career (so far) without the need to justify, or make sense of, how you got to where you are now. Instead, you are choosing to familiarise yourself with the unfiltered details of your career, and as you do, you aim to become skilled at understanding more of the details. As you do so, do not allow yourself to be mean or nasty, or allow your inner critic to get carried away. No, your focus is to delve into the zeitgeist to capture the realistic themes and events that combine to reveal what got you to where you are today. That information is made up of data from your past and present, and in this chapter you get to time travel between these two spaces to gain deeper insight into your career to date.

Raw and unfiltered – your Career Selfie

Your Career Selfie is a raw and honest snapshot of where you are in your career, your work and your life at this moment in time. It may be exactly the picture you expected and wanted, or it may not be, and you may want to move on swiftly. So, with your Permission Mindset activated, allow yourself to acknowledge whatever your experience is, good, bad or indifferent.

It is only through taking time to pause and reflect that you put yourself in a position to ask and answer critical questions. It is these critical questions, applied to your Career Selfie, that put you in a position of relative agency over that career story. I intentionally use the word 'relative' because there are very few of us with complete agency over any aspect of our lives, work or careers. We are so often making choices between several options, and choosing the one that fits best, or the lesser of two evils.

My partner of 21 years would love nothing more than to stop doing his work as a quantity surveyor. Don't get me wrong, he enjoys it, and he works with a great bunch of clients, but if he had complete agency, if money and the income that his business generates didn't matter, then he would work less hours, indulge his interest in trading stocks, and we would travel more. In reality, his agency is tempered during this season of his life by the need to work for an income. Yes, he has a career, but he must also work. The time will come when that changes, but for now he is not in a position of agency to do exactly as he wants. Now, there are things over which he does have control, and he has made small tweaks to how and where he works to manage this.

For example, if he must travel for work, he does so for one long day per week. This might mean he's away from home for 14–16 hours on that day, but for the rest of the week he's home for dinner, bedtimes and school collections.

While on the road, he listens to podcasts by investors and thought leaders on topics such as electric vehicles and cryptocurrencies. Over the past few years, he has built a small investment portfolio, and each week he spends time trading or educating himself. It's not perfect, but for now, during this season of his life, it is enough. Looking from the outside in, you would never think these were his feelings. He smiles (most of the time), works hard, does a great job and delivers with an attention to detail that I find myself consistently in awe of.

By taking a Career Selfie, he has developed an understanding of his 'why'. This placed him in a position of choice over the elements of his career that are within his control, rather than sacrificing and resenting those aspects he is unable to control. He hasn't sugar-coated it, and nor should you; the aim here is not to become unnecessarily positive but to better understand your Career Selfie. This understanding lays a practical and solid foundation upon which to understand your present, so that you can make choices now that build towards a future sustainable career, one in which you can thrive, flourish and progress.

Looking at the big picture to assess where you are now and what got you to here allows you to plan, piece by piece, for the next developmental phase of your career.

A word of warning

This chapter is a little different from the others. Your focus shifts from what happened before to what is happening now. This is often a tricky transition, the part of the career coaching process that people really get stuck in and want to give up.

If this is the case for you, I don't blame you. This is hard. Making the decision to confront where you are in this moment can bring up big feelings or thoughts. Likely you are already aware of these feelings and thoughts, but you are managing to swallow them most of the time, or at the very least contain them.

When I think about this, I remember my time working in that role early in my career. At the time a Career Selfie was exactly what I needed, but I always found an excuse – something small I liked about the role, or the fact that I had great colleagues. Equally, toxic positivity crept in to convince me that it wasn't that bad, and that others had it worse. And yes, others did have it worse, but that wasn't a good reason for staying in a job that was making me sick. The fear of what others would think or what others would say was a big part of it, judgement for not being able to 'stick it out'. And then there were the financial worries that came with leaving a permanent pensionable job.

The list of reasons not to take that Career Selfie were logical and understandable. I didn't want to deal with reality and I feared making choices. However, I missed the entire point of the Career Selfie. Engaging in the process does not necessarily mean that you must move to action. Taking a Career Selfie is just that, an honest snapshot in the moment of the what, where and why of your work and career. Nothing else. It is not a plan, and it does not require change or action. It might lead to a plan that brings change, and to achieve this you may need to act, but that is maybe for later, not for now.

Pause for 60

The aim of this Pause for 60 is to take a snapshot of your career in time. This is an unedited, unfiltered, realistic picture of you, taken by you. No grand gestures, no puppy dog ears.

Using Pause for 60 as a moment of reflection, get your pen and notebook and prepare to ask and answer the following question:

Where am I in my career now?

A run-of-the-mill question, this relates to your current role, industry and position. It should also include membership of professional bodies, continuous professional development and any facts about your future career progression in this role.

As you answer this question, stick to facts, and refrain from adding in emotions or feelings. That doesn't mean that you should stop yourself from having those emotions or feelings – acknowledging them is not just vital, it is the right thing to do, so feel the feelings, but for now, only record the facts; we are on a fact-finding mission.

Your answer reveals the current reality of your career, and will look something like this:

> I am a chartered accountant working in one of the Big Four as a senior financial advisor with specialist industry knowledge in the aviation industry. I am 15 years in the finance industry, nine of which are within the aviation industry and five of which I spent working in this firm.
>
> Prior to that, I joined [name of company or organisation] as a graduate. I then moved to the Emirates for three years before transferring back home to my current role in my current organisation.

Use this version to guide your thoughts:

> I am a member of the [name of professional body]. I am on track to become [name of position] within the next two years. My career progression plan is supported by two senior colleagues.
>
> Since joining I have completed [name(s) of professional courses]. I contribute to [name of network(s)] and I am an active member of [name of committee(s)].

Discipline yourself and for now, stick to the facts of your career.

Blurred reality – function or environment?

Playing to your cognitive strengths of getting information in easy-to-access bite-sized chunks, for now you are separating the core function of your role from your work environment. This might seem arbitrary, and it is, but it is also important for a number of reasons. A point we often miss about our career is that sometimes when we want change, we look in the wrong place. Our vision is blurred, it affects our reality, and by extension how we make decisions.

The fact is that the environment and the function of our career are so intertwined that when we think about our career it is often hard to tell one from the other. As you unravel the strands of your current career, the function of what you do, and the environment that you do it in, gradually become clearer as to which areas need your attention. For some it will be the function of what you do; for others it is the environment that you do it in; and for still others it will be a combination of both.

At first it may seem challenging to separate the function of what you do from the environment that you do your work in, as both are intertwined. That feeling is your reaction to the reality that when we think about work the link between function and environment is seldom separated, and naturally so. Your brain chunks together information about life so that you don't have to make an indiscriminate number of decisions each second of each day. The chunking prevents you from becoming overwhelmed.

For the purposes of fully exploring your present career story, it is important to dechunk, to take each piece of the puzzle, one piece at a time, and separate it from the rest. This step is essential in allowing your brain to cope with single pieces of information first, before it deals with the entirety of that information.

It is for these reasons that it is helpful to first examine

these aspects of your career in isolation. As you progress deeper into this chapter, you will begin to search for any points at which the function of your role and the environment in which you perform it cross over. Also, consider any points of divergence – perhaps where an aspect of what you like in the function of your role is muddied by the environment in which you do it, and takes away from your enjoyment of your role.

Let's think big but act small as we go. Clarity through collection of unfiltered information is the aim of our game at this point. As we progress, this data becomes the building blocks upon which you craft a sustainable career.

Lisa's story

For example, Lisa, a client I once worked with, was struggling in her role as an early career accountant. All through college and training she enjoyed her role, but since starting to work for one of the big firms, a dream realised, she discovered that accountancy wasn't for her. She came to me determined to change career and wanted to figure out what came next. As she took a Career Selfie and took a deep dive into exploring the function of her role versus her environment, it quickly became apparent that she still enjoyed the day-to-day of her work as an accountant. The function of her role still pleased her. In fact, she felt really engaged and had a sense of flow when doing her core work. This was an important revelation, as it provided vital information going forward.

Clarity – your function

As we attempt to arrive at a place of clarity of thought in your career, let's first focus on the functions of your work and career, the fundamental parts of your role. Day to day, this refers to the components of your role, the tasks that you do and the practical elements of your job. As you think about your core function, start to include the skills and competencies you exercise frequently. It might help to reflect on completed projects or daily tasks.

As you do this, be alert to the possibility that your core functions may not reflect your title, the job that you were hired for or the one that you trained for. This frequently happens, but is usually overlooked. You are so busy performing your career to the best of your ability that slowly, over time, things get added to or taken away from you, one small added responsibility followed by another change, and this eventually adds up to the point where suddenly you are doing a job that you barely recognise.

You might be happy with how things have turned out, or you may not. Either way, don't judge yourself harshly; this process is non-judgmental of others and of yourself.

Pause for 60

In this Pause for 60 you are concentrating on gaining clarity on the core day-to-day activities of your role and, by extension, your career. As you put pen to paper, record the things that you do, the roles that you play, and the practical aspects of what you do each and every day.

Collating this data affords you the opportunity to get into the detail of the job that you are currently doing and what it is, if anything, about that job that connects to your chosen career. The detail that emerges from this short burst of writing is often very telling.

So with pen in hand, and your notebook open, begin to record the function of your role at this moment in time.

Clarity – your environment

Your work environment, simply put, is the spaces you work in and, more importantly, the people who share those spaces with you. Whether your environment is virtual, remote, hybrid or office-based, it can be loosely defined as the primary location where you do your work.

Added to that is the mix of your colleagues you work with daily, the team(s) you interact with, the people in leadership. It also includes key stakeholders in your organisation, who might be customers or clients you deal with, contractors or consultants who offer bespoke services, or people from government departments or regulating or funding agencies.

This is a list of people you share these spaces with, and it is likely that it is a wide and varied one. Some of these people may be daily collaborators, others occasional connections, while still others are linked through a dotted line, or are never present but are influential. As you can see, it does not always have to be the people you work with directly or daily.

Pause for 60

The aim in this Pause for 60 is to concentrate on your work environment. You know best who is involved with you in your environment and the impact they each have on you, your role, your function and your career.

In this Pause for 60, include them.

Deirdre's story

Take the example of Deirdre, who was a lawyer at one of the leading law firms in the country. She apprenticed in the firm before working her way through the ranks, and was on target for partnership. Specialising in international corporate law, she thrived in her role and really loved what she did, but gradually a feeling of discontent arose. She went to her doctor to address a pattern of poor sleep that was developing, and to get her bloods done.

Over time she began to question every aspect of her job, from who she worked with to her industry as a whole, to the point that she started to consider other career options. As she engaged in the process of separating the function of her job from the environment she was doing it in, she identified previously missed patterns.

In the past couple of years, a senior lawyer who had mentored her had left the organisation. Previously, she had gone to that person for advice, to temperature-check and to bounce ideas. What she hadn't realised was that, when that person left the organisation, the buffer she provided between a very demanding senior leader and the more junior lawyers was removed. When she left the business, Deirdre was exposed directly, for the first time, to the management style of that senior leader. At the same time, she also lost daily and direct access to her mentor. While they remained in touch, the water cooler chats and the spontaneous lunches no longer happened.

Deirdre had learned her trade and worked through the ranks in this organisation. She had met some of her closest friends there, and even her life partner. Initially, Deirdre questioned if she was in the right career at all, but as she engaged in the process it transpired that it was the impact of the change in relationship and her direct reporting line that made the most difference. Her environment was the issue, no the function of her role.

Through coaching, Deirdre developed a strategy to manage and cope with the management style of her new manager. She put a strategy in place, and as she did, she excelled in her role. She has now made the next step in her role towards partner in that organisation, and has negotiated a sabbatical to gain experience in a global HQ of the same organisation in a different country.

This is an example of an environmental work issue that, if unexplored, has the potential to derail a career plan by focusing on the function of your role, rather than the actual issue at hand. Deirdre was considering a nuclear option, and was questioning whether law was for her at all, such was the impact that it was having on her well-being. While she might have found happiness in a different career, the issue was not the function of her role, but her environment.

How do you feel?

Now that you have established the facts and collated the data, it's time to think about your feelings and thoughts around the what, where and who. Up to this point emotions and feelings were left out intentionally, and this was done for several reasons, but mainly to help your brain function optimally, by dissecting information into smaller pieces that you can reassemble in the future.

This might be something of an emotional rollercoaster. Again, there is no right or wrong way to react, there is your way, so whatever that is, with your Permission Mindset activated, allow yourself your own reaction. Thinking again about your role, function and environment, what are your feelings and thoughts?

Trust your gut on this. Be honest with your emotions, let them tumble out and onto the page. They may at first appear to make no sense, but remember, feelings are not binary; they occur on a spectrum ranging from awful to amazing and everything in between. It is unlikely that you will be on the same end of the spectrum every day. What is more likely is that your feelings will reflect a range of emotions. While you might not like one part of your role, you might really like another; about others you might feel indifferent. Do this same exercise in a year, and you might look at your career through a different lens.

Remember, we are looking for raw and unfiltered clarity in this moment, with no fancy self-editing.

Pause for 60

In this Pause for 60, use the information that you have collated so far about the functional and environmental aspects of your role. As you grab your pen and paper, ask yourself, When I think about the functional and environmental aspects of my career, role, position and industry:

- How do I feel?
- What do I think?
- What happens within me?
- What feelings arise or emotions are triggered?
- On a scale of 1–10, what is the impact of the core function of my role on other parts of my life and well-being? (1 = very negative, 10 = very positive)
- When I look at the people I work with, my managers and leaders, do I feel inspired to be like them?
- Do I feel valued, included in decision-making and have a sense of belonging within my team and the wider organisation?
- Do I feel treated fairly, with dignity and respect? Are others treated fairly, and with dignity and respect?
- When I look at those in hierarchical positions of power, does that table reflect the principles of fairness, equality, dignity and respect? If so, how? If not, how?

- Do I have the opportunity to progress in my career in a meaningful way within the organisation?
- What are the organisational policies on well-being, caring and parenting, work–life balance and flexible work?
- Do I feel a sense of entitlement to access these policies, or does it feel like there is a gap between what the policy says and what happens in practice? Is there friction between the lived reality of the policy and written documents? Is this just on my team or is it across the organisation?
- How do I feel about the values of the company and the organisational culture? Do the values of the organisation, my industry and my role align with my values?

These are not easy questions to answer, but they are fundamental in understating your now so that you can craft a future sustainable career. If you need more time, or feel like continuing at this point, do so. This is your career, and your future, so do what you need to do for yourself.

Time off and career dedication

Annual paid leave is a statutory entitlement, enshrined in and protected by law through statutory provision in Ireland and protected by European Union directives. Most countries offer protection for annual leave, although the amount of time offered varies from region to region.[3]

Annual leave is vital to our well-being; it allows time for repair, recovery and relaxation, the opportunity to take control over your time, to use it to engage in joyful activities. Spending time in the presence of people we love who make us smile cannot be overestimated. Research backs this up, and shows that annual leave is positively related to optimal functioning and overall well-being.[4]

So important is time off, not just annual leave, that many companies offer increased benefits depending on your hierarchical level within an organisation. Recently, it has become fashionable, as a recruitment and wellness strategy, to introduce unlimited paid time off (UPTO). UPTO affords a person the opportunity to take whatever time off they need, no questions asked, once your work is done, in order to take care of life outside of work. The real perk comes when this leave is full pay and with an unlimited amount of time off.

Despite the growth in devices, platforms and technology that promise to make us more productive in smaller frames of time, the lack of free time that we report having has reduced rather than increased. Are UPTOs then the antidote to our collective 'time famine'?

Over the past two decades, through some sort of tragic paradox, while we have developed clever ways of saving time, the demands of our jobs and time pressure have increased. The outcome is that people feel pushed to work faster and longer to meet deadlines. This is particularly the case for workers in service or knowledge-intensive industries. In these roles, problem-solving, knowledge-sharing, creativity and interpersonal teamwork are highly valued commodities.

The novel innovations demanded as outputs of this type of knowledge work defied the spatial and temporal boundaries traditionally associated with work and life. As these boundaries collapsed, so too did the ability to switch off. Often referred to as the 'squeezed middle', these highly educated, high-income workers frequently feel strapped for cash despite that high income, and they have become accustomed to spending time, even spare time, a scarce commodity, in increasingly efficient ways.

The underpinning aim of UPTO is to improve well-being,

motivation, health and performance outcomes of employees at the individual, team and organisational levels. However, early research into this new workplace phenomenon, by *Frontiers in Psychology*, published in 2022, reveals the lived reality of UPTO to be very different. This research raises the question, does UPTO 'unlock the best, or unleash the beast'? In practice, does this seemingly brilliant perk translate into actionable and concrete actions that lead to solutions for the time-starved worker?[5]

It depends on the organisation, individual and team. This may work well for some, providing the perfect antidote to time issues. For others, the freedom to choose when or if to take time off presents a barrier to taking any time off at all. So instead of workers taking annual leave they take no time off, for fear of appearing unengaged or uncompetitive. For some people, such as contractors or those on zero-hours contracts, availing of such benefits could result in loss of employment or create the fear of losing your job. Particularly in industries that value high time commitment, prize visibility and already have high incidences of burnout, the sense of entitlement of workers to access this new perk is limited, and therefore has the potential to have the opposite of its intended effect.

So where does this leave us?

You may find yourself going down a rabbit hole as you engage with these questions, but they are worth exploring. In a world where time is so precious, we seldom get the space to think about how, where, when or with whom we spend our 168 hours per week. When we try to take that time, it can feel overwhelming, as it is hard to know where to start or what to do.

During this phase of crafting your sustainable career it is vital that you give yourself permission to examine environmental factors that may in fact be determining how you spend your time. Time intensification is often taken for granted, as just the way things are, but it doesn't have to be so. Different industries, smaller organisations and role changes can make all the difference. Stick with the process, and as you go through each stage, what may at first appear as clear as mud will become gradually more visible.

Context – the world around you matters

Without a doubt, there are sociocultural, personal and contextual factors that have impacted the way you have performed your career so far. In all likelihood, choosing not to think like a career critic with regard to the external factors that impact your career has also been important in your understanding of your story so far. What I mean by this is it is our tendency to fall into the default 'Well this is just the way things are' thinking.

This is not your fault. We are taught how to behave if we are to be accepted. This happens in our families, homes, schools and places of work. People may claim that being critical or asking questions is welcomed, but let's be clear, it's generally not really appreciated.

With this in mind, we are choosing to think and reflect on the reality of our career at this very moment in time. Remember, don't be hard on yourself. This is not about blame, it's about understanding so that you can connect the dots between your past and present and create a story for your future sustainable career.

Once you have collected the facts, it's time to think about what you enjoy about these facts. What is it about what you do that brings you joy? Why is it that you stay in the job, role or industry? Using a very specific lens, you are considering if you are caught by the salary, the perks or the title. I remember staying in a job with a high-end retailer because

I really liked being able to say that I worked there, and we got a 50 per cent discount on gorgeous clothes. The rate of pay was less than my friends got working in either of the large German discount stores, but I liked the title and the perks. At the time I justified my position by saying the hours suited better, but that wasn't really true.

Pause for 60

What about you? You might enjoy travelling with your work, or the flexible, hybrid or remote work patterns. It might be the office you have, or the car parking space. Pause for 60 and reflect on whatever it is that you like or enjoy about your role, level or industry. Name them.

Once you have finished, it's time to flip the coin and consider the least appealing aspects of your role, industry or level. Remember, there are no right or wrong ways to answer these questions. This is your career, and therefore what is included as the reasons for liking or disliking something must be written in accordance with your script and story.

At this stage you have your pros and cons on paper. You have outlined your role, function and industry, what you like and what you dislike. This is the big-picture information. As you complete this section you may find your brain hooked by job advert buzzwords, words such as resilience, team player or creative. However, your focus is more personal than that. Activate your Permission Mindset and remind yourself that this is your career and your life. Including generic buzzwords to describe you fails to capture the unique contribution that you make.

Focus on understanding the things you do well, really well, each and every day. This might include attention to detail or open communication. Focus is important here, as we try to shape your Career Selfie. Your focus is on understanding what you do, and how you do it so that you can integrate your now into your future sustainable career.

At this point you have committed to paper the function of your role, and within that you will have begun to identify the skills and competencies that you have learned and earned. You may begin to see the outline of your story unfold as your brain triggers into action and starts to piece parts of the puzzle together.

Jim's story

Jim worked in an organisation that lobbied government organisations to move to action on environmental and humanitarian issues. Jim loved his role and felt that he was genuinely making a difference to the lives of others, both now and in the future. He could see that governments, based on the research and development work his organisation did, were taking a stand and resourcing more green and sustainable policies.

After Jim had spent 15 months in his role, his organisation was acquired by a large multinational. The purpose of the acquisition was complex, but from what he understood the purchasing organisation could now offset carbon credits against its own carbon footprint. On further investigation, Jim found that the acquiring organisation held another business that designed, developed and sold military equipment, including bombs, to countries led by those who held different ideological and political beliefs than he did.

Upon realising this, how Jim felt about his job changed fundamentally. Remember, his job had not changed in any way; the day-to-day of his function remained fundamentally the same. Additionally, his direct team and managers remained the same. What changed was the wider environment within which he worked, and this led to a feeling of moral compromise.

The acquisition affected how Jim felt about his co-workers. He had enjoyed a great working relationship with the small team he was part of. However, when these facts became clear, many of the team didn't care about the acquisition, or the role that the acquiring company played in international war. Jim couldn't rationalise this, and he became increasingly stressed, anxious and angry.

The acquisition for Jim was a deal breaker, but one that he struggled to understand fully prior to completing this exercise. As he better understood his Career Selfie, he placed himself in a position of agency. He no longer felt a lack of control over his circumstances, nor did he fear what he would do next. Until this point, the only thing he had considered was to quit immediately, but he knew that this wasn't a realistic option, as he depended on his wage to pay his rent and to live. He felt paralysed; he needed clarity. Really understanding the issues at play made a significant difference for Jim.

Now, armed with the information he needed to make choices based on what was within his control, he could move from thought to action. Based on this information he developed an exit strategy from his workplace. As he did this, he began to make practical decisions about the steps he could take over the coming months that would lead to a new job that aligned with his values.

What to do with what you now know

As you re-examine all the information about your career up till now, what is your reaction? Is this where you thought you would be during this season of your career? Do you feel you have achieved what you want? Have you realised your ambitions? Do you know what success looks like to you?

These are big questions, and without doubt it is easier to sidestep them. Making the decision to not answer them is gratifying in the moment but in the long term it offers you few, if any, options. As we begin to think about how we might best use this information, it is time to shift our focus from what we know to what we think we might want.

This is the exciting part, when we begin to explore the possibility in the future. This is the phase of your unfiltered deep dive in which you grant yourself permission to ignore the practicalities and rules that we are so often held back by and begin to design success by you and for you. It is where you begin to lay the foundations for your sustainable career story. Yes, some of this might feel like you are dreaming, but let's not fool ourselves, the only dreams that become plans, capable of being realised, are those that are committed to paper.

But first – the illusion of control

It is also important that at this juncture we discuss agency. For some time now, popular opinion has suggested that, once you set your mind to it, anything is possible. Research refers to this phenomenon as the 'illusion of control', whereby we believe we have more agency and control over uncontrollable outcomes in our lives than we really do. There are many reasons that we may do this, chief among them self-preservation! The illusion of control serves as a self-esteem-enhancing mechanism that allows us to take credit for any positive outcomes, like a promotion or a raise, but attribute failures to external factors.

And yes, there is a truthful element in that, but often circumstance and context combine to present factors that are outside of your control, and as a result erect barriers of varying complexity. The idea of working at a side hustle, for example, all the while working full-time, to build a business that affords you the opportunity to leave that full-time role, and earn enough money to survive and thrive, is possible, and there are examples of many who have done so against the odds.

But we must normalise the conversation to include the notion that working such long hours typically means that you have the time to do so. This likely means that you don't have caring or rearing responsibilities, and if you do that you have a partner and/or a support network who share the load with you so that you can dedicate yourself to your side hustle. It also suggests that you are financially comfortable, perhaps having access to someone with money, upon whom you can rely if things go poorly or if something unexpected happens.

If you are in this position, please don't feel judged; in fact quite the opposite. As a mother of four children under the age of 10 I defy the statistics. I am an outlier, an anomaly in the world of working mothers. I am, however, also a statistic.

I work shorter hours than my partner, I left the paid workforce after my first baby and I left my full-time role to enter precarious self-employment. While employment status, hours and wages rarely change for a man upon the arrival of a child, that is simply not the case for women. An Understanding Society 2018 report found that 17 per cent of women leave paid employment completely in the five years following childbirth, in comparison to just 4 per cent of fathers.[6] This study also revealed that the number of children did not increase the likelihood that a woman would return to employment, but rather her employment status in the year before childbirth. Research in the UK reviewing inequalities identified that female employment rates drop sharply from 90 per cent to 75 per cent after a mother's first child. This is not to mention the rate at which her wage will fall as she is placed on the 'mommy track' that we discussed earlier in the book.

As I work outside the home in self-employment, we struggled to get a mortgage. We were told that, had I been a full-time stay-at-home mother, it would have been easier to secure a mortgage. My husband, it was explained, would benefit from my tax credits, and if I stayed at home, we would have had no childcare costs.

The reality is that working in paid or unpaid work presents an ongoing negotiation and renegotiation of the working world, your relationships with others and the rules upon which it is built. It includes dealing with the taxation system, access to adequate childcare, navigating the education system and affordable medical care. This in turn requires a really thick skin in order to cope with the comments and remarks about being selfish for working while you have young children, the lack of time to do anything and the idea that once you are a mother you should enter into some sort of state of selfless perfection in which you put the needs of everyone, including your partner, ahead of yours. And as you do so it is incumbent upon you to perform your role quietly, with humility and without complaint. In fact, you are advised to lean into the broken system, one that makes it almost impossible for you to navigate, to have a sustainable career, to enjoy life.

Let's be clear, this system denies everyone the right to a sustainable career while enjoying life. Success is defined and designed according to parameters that belong to a different era. I have a partner who shares my personal and professional ambitions. This was not a natural journey for us, and it is something that we have had to work really hard on. After we became parents we had to recontract and renegotiate our relationship. Our lives and our careers became interconnected and interdependent on each other in a way that they previously were not. For either one of us to go to work, to travel or to work late it meant that we had to consult the other. While we always chatted about work and what we were doing before, there was never a requirement for either one of us to be in a specific place at a specific time, otherwise our little baby would be the last person leaving crèche that evening.

It is important, however, to remember that we're not all in the same position, and it is unfair to send messages that suggest that people who can't make changes to navigate towards a sustainable career are in some way at fault, that they could do it if they just worked harder, were more committed, could build more resilience or just toughened up. Many people are simply not able to give one more ounce of anything, either emotionally or physically.

What does success mean to you?

As you enter this next phase of self-reflection, consider what perfect would look like for you, What does success mean to you during this season of your life? Success is a loaded term, and one we often fear. Let's start by attempting to define it by you, for you.

When you think about success, what comes to mind? Based on that, how do you measure success? These are not questions we ask very often and, given the chance, you, just like me, will often try to sidestep them. If we are truly honest with ourselves, most of us are not sure what our definition of success is. Instead, we tend to look to friends, family, peers, work colleagues, business leaders or influencers to help us define the parameters of our personal version of success. We become so wrapped up in the business of life that we suddenly find that the idea of success we've been pursuing feels uncomfortable and somehow doesn't fit our needs.

Ask yourself: If everything in my life now was perfect, what would that look like? Don't be afraid to delve into the detail. Be descriptive and clear about what you really want. A great friend of mine, who is an HR thought leader, once said to a group of mothers about to return to work, 'Ask for what you want and not what you think you will get.' This really struck me. So often, what we ask for in life is tempered by what we think others expect of us, or what we think we are entitled to. The result is that we ask for half of what we really want and end up with less than we deserve. We downplay our ambitions and our desires. We worry that, by asking for what we want, we might upset someone else, might rock the boat.

Remember, at this stage, we are exploring, thinking and describing. This is unedited and free-form. It provides the building blocks for what will come later, as you get into the detail of your sustainable career story on paper. It doesn't mean that you must do anything right away. It is the start of the process, a beginning point.

So as you answer the questions that follow, activate your Permission Mindset and, with an open mind, allow yourself to describe what you really want, not what you think you should get. Give yourself permission to put on paper what you mean by success during this season of your life. There is no single answer, just as there is no right answer. The secret to a sustainable career is understanding what you need and how you define success according to that.

Pause for 60

What would success look like in my life, work and career during this season of my life? Here are some questions to start you off:

- What would I have more time for?
- What would I have less time for?
- What strengths would I get to use?
- What skills and expertise would I exercise?
- What would motivate, engage and fulfil me?
- What would my workday look like, e.g. remote work, flexitime, a short commute or more travel?

- How much money would I earn?
- What would I say no to that I currently say yes to?
- What people currently in my life would I choose not to engage with any more?

As you think about these questions, other questions will begin to present themselves. Some of these will come equipped with immediate answers. Others will present a puzzle and their answers will come more slowly as you think about them more deeply. This is an exciting phase. It is the part of the process where you get to dream on paper, explore and think about options and ideas for what is next. It is your opportunity to let go of expectations and rules that would otherwise limit your thinking.

As you begin to arrive at a definition of success designed by you, for you, it becomes increasingly apparent what season of life you are in, and what is important to you during this time. This definition of success as it evolves paves the way for you to establish your boundaries, upon which you build that version of success.

Pause for 60

Pause for 60 and ask yourself the following questions:

- What season of my life am I currently in?
- Am I working or do I have a career?
- Is this where I thought I would be?
- Am I happy with where I am?

- If so, why?
- If not, why not?
- What actions that were within my control got me here?
- What role did I play in getting to where I am?

At first glance, these questions appear simple, but let me tell you, when you really dig down into the core of these questions, you gain some powerful information.

CHAPTER 8
What You Can Learn From MacGyver

'Who do you love, Mammy?'
– My daughter, aged 5

I was standing at the end of my kitchen island, being grilled by a small and relentless interrogator:

'Who do you love, Mammy?'

'Well, I love you, your sisters, your dad.' (Our fourth baby was not born at this point.)

'Anyone else?'

'Well, yes, our family and friends.'

Not satisfied with large groups labelled broadly, she demanded more detail:

'But *who* do you mean?'

I proceeded to expertly name 50 or so people, starting with brothers and sisters, along with their partners and children, followed by both sets of grandparents. Next I moved on to our friends, before concluding with our children's friends, confident that the list was complete.

Still unsatisfied, my hazel-eyed, pig-tailed inquisitor said, 'You forgot someone. Who did you forget?'

It was the end of a long day at home with two small kids

and a 12-week-old baby. I was getting ready to speak at an event that required an overnight stay. Our baby and my husband were coming along as I was exclusively breastfeeding.

'No,' I said, my tone betraying that my patience with this line of questioning was reaching near breaking point, 'I *have not.*' As far as I was concerned, I had covered everyone bar the postman. But according to my five-year-old, *someone* was missing.

'You have!' she insisted.

'Who?' I asked.

With a toothless smile and a leg hug, she announced, 'What about you, Mammy? You forgot the most important person in the world – you never said you love yourself.'

I was floored. I did forget myself. I forgot to say, 'I love me.' I had in fact thought of the postman before I considered putting myself on that list.

And I blame MacGyver!

The MacGyver Fallacy

Do you remember the TV show *MacGyver*? The 1980s action thriller following the life of a secret agent who, armed with infinite scientific knowledge, a Swiss army knife and duct tape, saves the world, repeatedly? Fuelled by a strong sense of social justice, he achieved incredible feats seemingly without ever sleeping, eating or drinking. We watched as, at the end of a long day, the closing scene usually, he would head off into the sunset, alone, with the flames of success glowing behind. MacGyver was 100 per cent committed to his job for the Phoenix Foundation. Over the years the show aired, we learned little about his life, relationships or interests. He was what we might now call a workaholic, earnest in his devotion to his work, and only his work. This is what I refer to as the MacGyver Fallacy.

MacGyver was the quintessential hero who powers through, keeps going no matter what and, most importantly, never gives up. He is tough, resilient, committed, focused and kind. He is also in great physical shape and mentally tough to boot. That story, the one where we are told to 'power through', 'lean in', 'just keep going', 'don't give up' has conditioned us all. So much so that we tend to think, 'If I'm productive, then I will feel good, and when I feel good, I will feel well.' This persuasive social narrative has resulted in flawed thinking that sees productivity being valued more highly than basic human well-being.

Really, is it any wonder that we are getting sick from overwork and that we struggle to set boundaries? Or, perhaps more profoundly, that we are so busy doing that we forget to love ourselves?

You are not MacGyver – nor any other action hero or brilliant professional who, to achieve success, must sacrifice everything else.

Lost in the doing – the role of technology

Technology has played its part in this perfect storm. Compared even to just 15 years ago we each have seamless access to devices that, in theory, help us to achieve more in less time, to be efficient and, overall, more productive. These machines with unique operating systems are designed, developed and built to run at capacity 24/7. Yes, they might need to be charged or updated, but once you do that, apart from the odd glitch, they tend to operate optimally. In turn, we are provided with non-stop access to information, each other and the wider world.

We are not programmed to live, work or operate this way. As humans, we need rest, sleep and downtime to function; without it we crash and become unwell. So what is well-being, and how can we get some? In its simplest form, well-being is feeling well enough to experience health, happiness and prosperity as you live your life. More specifically, it is the ability to feel good and function effectively, as you navigate the highs and lows of work and life consistently. It includes good mental health, high life satisfaction, a sense of meaning and purpose and the ability to manage stress. This doesn't mean that you must exist in a constant state of happiness – that is impossible and unhealthy. The aim is to be well enough to experience feelings, to feel happy and content 80 per cent of the time, and to be able to cope with the 20 per cent of the time that life is challenging.

When we feel physically, emotionally, socially and professionally well, we engage in a mutually enhancing cycle in which we:

- Have more energy
- Feel connected to ourselves and others
- Have more focus and motivation
- Are more productive at work.

It is possible to increase your well-being by developing a few simple, practical and science-backed techniques. First off, you must make your well-being a priority. While this may feel and sound counter-intuitive, remember the oxygen mask on the plane analogy: unless you help yourself first, you will not be able to help anyone else, even the most important people in your life. Deciding what parts of your well-being are most important, and where you are going to focus your time and energy, is vital. Your non-negotiables are the clear, well-defined themes upon which your well-being exists.

Yet somehow, as more and more time was freed up by technology, we have become more and more time-poor at worst, or time-stretched at best. We feel busier than ever, and most of us are in pursuit of work–life balance, where work and life sit in perfect harmony. But frequently that quest feels like a journey to find the leprechaun with the pot of gold at the end of the rainbow – each time you appear to be almost there, the elusive end of the rainbow shifts and, as if by magic, you never reach it.

The graduate who quit before he started

Not long ago I was chatting to a recent graduate who worked for a global law firm, who explained that he was leaving for a similar role in a smaller organisation, and doing so for significantly less pay. In fact, to make it work, he was moving back into his family home. When I asked why, he told me this story: 'I was leaving work about two Fridays ago around 6 p.m. The office was still busy, but I had my work done and knock-off time is 5.30, so I decided to go home. On my way out, I bumped into my boss, who said, "See you tomorrow." I said, "Not tomorrow, mate, it's Saturday." Then he walked alongside me for a few steps on the footpath beside the canal and told me, "If you want to make it here you really need to show an interest and be more visible after hours and on weekends. This is your second week not coming in on Saturday and leaving on Friday evening, and you know these things are noticed. It's good fun here on the weekends. It's laid back and we kinda enjoy it. The days are short; if you're in around ten, you get home before four, unless it's a very busy week.'

That was all he needed to hear. On the way home that evening, he made the decision to leave. His boss, in his mid-40s, was a lovely man and a brilliant professional who showed great kindness to his team. He was also overweight, and had spent time in hospital the previous year with a TIA (a transient ischaemic attack, or what is often called a 'ministroke'). He was a dad of three who typically worked a 70-hour week.

My graduate friend went on to say, 'I really don't know

when he sees his kids, and we heard on the grapevine that his marriage is in trouble. I looked at him and saw a future I didn't like, so I decided to make the change now, rather than wait until I was so dependent on the money that I couldn't leave.' That job was a greedy job, in a greedy organisation that lives and breathes the MacGyver Fallacy. People are treated as resources, counted in numbers and are considered dispensable if their operating system isn't able to fully commit to the role. That commitment is shown through availability for work all day, every day.

As you read this, you may think that people have a role to play, and that we should just learn to say no. But when faced with these situations, the balance of power is too often tipped in favour of the organisation, and if it emerges that you are not a cultural fit, well then, you are in trouble. We know that industries with 100 per cent billable hours policies, including consultancy, financial services and the legal world, are notorious for weeding out the weak ones in the early years. The tech industry is likewise renowned for a work ethic that requires you to always be on and available.

Before we go any further, we repeat: you are not MacGyver, and you do not have an operating system with 24/7 capacity. You are a person who needs to eat, sleep, move and spend time with people who make you smile (including yourself), *as well as* having a career or going to work, not *instead of*. There is no amount of stress, resilience or productivity training that can teach you to be more MacGyver. This is a dangerous neoliberalist fallacy that we must uproot from our collective consciousness.

Wellness first – every time

The reality is that, if you want to be productive, you must first be well. In an always on and 100 per cent productivity at all costs culture, it can be hard to justify taking a few minutes to yourself during the workday. In fact, many of us struggle to take a full lunch hour, often having lunch at the desk. Working at 100 per cent capacity 100 per cent of the time is both unsustainable and impossible. Humans can't focus effectively for eight hours straight. Workplace practices that expect us to do so are illogical, counterproductive and ineffective. Research by a group of health scientists, led by professor of clinical exercise physiology Niall Moyna, found that sitting for eight hours a day, which equates to almost 80 per cent of our waking time, was as harmful to our health and well-being as smoking, leading to heart disease, obesity, diabetes and, in some cases, early death.[1]

If you want to achieve peak performance in any aspect of life, work or your career, your physical and mental well-being must be your first priority. It is not the role of one single individual to shift this narrative, it is in our power as a collective that we have the capacity to move the dial. And, as we do, it is incumbent upon organisations, organisational leaders and governments to put policies and procedures in place that give us the permission to blend work and life in a way that prevents sickness and lack of engagement.

Well-being is far more than a well-written policy and bananas in the canteen, it is a lived practice that filters from the top down. When people in a position of power and influence within an organisation don't practice what they preach, and when an organisation, through its stakeholders, holds people accountable for only maximising profit, people become numbers, and when that happens people get sick, and they leave the business.

The CFO who started to take lunch

I once worked with a CFO in the City of London. Referred by a colleague of mine, he came to me asking to collaborate on the design, development and delivery of an in-house pilot on career agility. This was a forward-thinking plan, because in 2014 this sort of career development was not as fashionable as it is today. In fact, when I set up this business from zero clients, my family and friends knew I went to work, but nobody really knew what I did.

In the early years, most of my work involved client-based one on ones for people who wanted to pivot in their career path. As time passed, those clients started to come back to ask me to work in-house to develop career agility programmes. Now, as I write this book, I have a thriving practice both online and in person, working in a business that supports myself and my family. Much has changed since those early days, and media attention on the area of careers since then has helped people to understand what I do.

But back to my CFO client. As part of any design collaboration, I spend many hours in discovery with the team I'm going to work with and their senior leaders. During the discovery period, I noticed a very high turnover rate in the team; in fact it was three times higher than the firm average. When I asked why this was, he told me that the turnover rate was the reason he wanted to pilot the career agility programme. He went on to tell me that several staff in their exit interviews had said that poor career development opportunities was their main reason for leaving.

I chatted to some of the longest-serving members of his team, to see what they had to say on the matter. They told me that the CFO was a brilliant boss, and a great leader who had the best interests of the team at heart, but that he was a workaholic, arriving at the office before 7 a.m. and staying past 7 p.m. He tended to have lunch at his desk, and he worked most Saturdays. This aside, he was very clear that the team needed to take breaks, avail of flexible work practices, and to finish up and start on time, but despite his words and kindness, his actions denied his team the permission to avail of these perks.

When I presented my proposal, the CFO was surprised and unimpressed. I had suggested a basic level-one health and well-being intervention. It was nothing to do with the carefully crafted career agility brief he shared with me. At the time I really needed the work, as I wanted to move into the corporate world, but not at any cost. In retrospect, I'm unsure if I was being brave, naïve or stupid. It was likely a mix of all three.

I told the CFO, the person who would sign my cheque if I got the job, that he needed to work on his non-negotiables before I could do any further work on a career agility programme with him or his team. I candidly explained that if he continued to work like this, despite putting in place a career agility programme, the high turnover rates would continue. I also suggested that he was running a high risk of burnout and that he would most likely end up sick. Perplexed, he simply couldn't get his head around what I was telling him. Leaving the detailed brief with him, I asked him to think about my suggestions and to chat to other professionals in his space.

After a three-week lag, I got a call. He told me he hated what I had said, but knew it needed to happen, and that he wanted to work on his non-negotiables. He decided to start off with two basic principles: he would leave the office every day for lunch, and three times a week he would go to the gym. He began to take his gym bag to work and, when leaving for the gym, he would throw his bag on his shoulder to signal to his team where he was going. This plan was carefully considered, and he understood the commitment involved.

I find that it takes three weeks to break a habit and a further three weeks to make a habit. Since habits are a learned behaviour formed through repetition, routine and ritual, they must be broken down before being rebuilt. A time frame of six weeks gives you the opportunity to put a plan in place and then break it into bite-sized changes that you can implement over the course of time. You will face challenges of discipline and motivation as you go through this process, but when you do, activate your Permission Mindset. Acknowledge that change is hard, and remind yourself that you are actively choosing to change because it is important to you.

So it was with the CFO. He decided to start small and agreed that he would work his way towards his goal. After 12 weeks of commitment to taking lunch and going to the gym, he began the process of reducing the length of his workday by starting later and finishing earlier. For the first week he came in at 7.15 a.m. and left at 6.45 p.m., and after that he shaved 15 minutes off his start and finish times piece by piece until he was starting work at 8.30 a.m. and finishing at 5.30 p.m.

This was manageable, and something he could scale. As a proud person, he didn't want to fail, and if he did, he certainly didn't want to do so publicly.

Tactical Thursday

Based on this, we made the decision that each week I would work as his weekly accountability partner, which we called 'Tactical Thursday'. In this weekly chat we worked through the following five questions:

1. What went well this week?
2. Where was the struggle?
3. What was within your control?
4. Who could you ask for help/support?
5. What is the smallest thing you could do differently next week to improve on this week?

Some weeks these questions were easy to answer, some weeks he didn't want to talk, and other weeks the progress was felt. A point of weekly self-reflection meant that things that were going well we incrementally developed on doing better. If on the other hand something was going poorly, a weekly check-in meant that it was acknowledged and dealt with before it derailed his end goal.

These simple changes, made over the course of the next six months, resulted in significant improvement. Team turnover decreased, and he noticed that projects were running on time, and that each team member started to hit their KPIs. He talked about a buzz in the team that hadn't been there before, and the reignited enjoyment he felt in his work.

Team members began to take lunch, start at a time that worked for them and finish on time, all while getting their work done. Work was now a place they enjoyed. This was not a coincidence; his changed behaviour showed his team his commitment to living the policies in place, not just talking about them. His actions gave his team permission to access the policies that up until then had lived on paper only.

Personally, he felt in the best shape of his life, and his relationship with his partner was renewed. They took a holiday with no work emails or phone calls, just the two of them. On that holiday they began to talk about surrogacy for the first time in years.

The plan was simple, the actions were intentional and he committed to them fully. Together, they formed his non-negotiables. And yes, we did also work on the career agility programme for his team. It ended in a programme that allowed his team members to take a six-month internal sabbatical to work as part of another business function or to take two years in another organisation safe in the knowledge that their job was open to them upon return. It also put in place access to upskilling, reskilling and retraining opportunities that were built into weekly work schedules.

This could never have happened had our CFO friend not worked on his non-negotiables first. If the foundations upon which he built that career agility programme had been rocky, the entire programme was destined to failure.

So what are non-negotiables, and how can you get them?

What are your non-negotiables?

Non-negotiables are the antidote to the MacGyver Fallacy and form the bedrock upon which a future sustainable career is possible. The purpose of your non-negotiables is to provide you with clear, well-defined pillars with which you craft the story of your sustainable career. Given what you now know about how we tend to think about, choose and engage with our careers, it should be clear that it is vital to have boundaries in place that protect what you want, need and desire in a sustainable career.

Once in place, your non-negotiables help manage stress, maintain your health and, in so doing, provide you with the physical and psychological space you need to thrive, not just survive, as you design a sustainable career. That said, it takes time to understand your own personal non-negotiables, and to put them in place. This is your opportunity to define your norms and to figure out what works for you.

Your non-negotiables exist in the grey space that sits at the intersection between your physical, personal and professional self. This dynamic trio of your physical, personal and professional non-negotiables together form a powerful decision-making platform. Combined, they are as unique as your fingerprint and speak to the people, skills, activities and challenges that give you a sense of contentment and happiness in your life, work and career. Once you have refined them it is possible to condense them into 15 or so words that act as reminders of your boundaries, needs and hopes.

Decision-making fatigue and your brain

As you know from our work in previous chapters, your brain likes to receive information, at least initially, in easy-to-digest, bite-sized chunks. This avoids information overload that can result in decision-making fatigue, which I bet you know all about, though you may not have a name for it.

A really common form of decision-making fatigue is impulse buying. Remember the last time you were in a shop and, instead of buying a banana, you bought a chocolate bar, a packet of crisps and a can of Coke? Equally, you weigh up all your options only to find that once you have all necessary information you become reluctant to make any decision at all, or you decide on one option but later regret it. If you experience this type of decision fatigue it is likely that you come up with your best ideas in the shower, while exercising or during your two-week summer holiday. When you have time and space to process you think more clearly and make better decisions.

If you are pushed to make a decision when in the throes of decision fatigue you tend to opt for a default decision. You do this subconsciously and make your choice based on the needs or opinions of others and society rather than making the right choice for you. Most likely you display an array of these behaviours at different times depending on the situation. If you do, this is your brain's way of asking you to please slow down, focus on a single task and give it the space to function optimally.

Decision-making fatigue happens after you have made so many decisions that your ability to make any additional decisions becomes negatively impacted. While the psychological effects of decision-making fatigue vary from person to person, you likely recognise some of the symptoms. Contributing causal factors in decision-making fatigue include repeated exposure to stress, a role that requires you to make lots of choices, particularly ones that significantly affect others, continuously completing tasks that require complex problem-solving, and lack of sleep.[2]

As you begin to think about crafting your non-negotiables, activate your Permission Mindset and give yourself the time and the space to let your brain function optimally. If you follow this process, your collective non-negotiables become a wildly powerful north star that will guide you as you design your sustainable career. Functioning as a daily reminder of your needs, they are the basis upon which you protect your yes and own your no. Your non-negotiables are a refined list of approximately 15 words, captured under what you will come to call your three Ps, or your physical, personal and professional non-negotiables. This task, though not necessarily easy, is inherently important and satisfying, and the rewards it brings infinitely outweigh the challenge.

There is no ready-made script for your non-negotiables, and when you have developed them they exist in a dynamic state that is constantly evolving. While some remain consistent over time, others shift depending on the season of your life, and there are no right or wrong answers to the question.

With that in mind, let's consider the first of your three Ps: your physical non-negotiables.

Physical non-negotiables

Physical non-negotiables are universal to everyone. There are few areas where the wider fields of psychology, science, nutrition, medicine and psychiatry agree, but this is one of them. Central to our survival is our shared basic need to eat, sleep, move and spend time with people, in order to function.

While slight variations within and between the broad pillars apply, each one of us, without exception, need these four core foundations built into the story of our sustainable career. Just like our CFO friend, who started off with understanding his physical non-negotiables, you too must do the same.

Your physical non-negotiables are the science-backed essentials, fundamental to the existence of all human life, yet so often they are the needs that we neglect, the impact of which is an unsustainable career, one with negative consequences that reach into all aspects of life. So slow and silent is the journey to neglecting these pillars of life that we often don't see it, only realising what has happened upon reaching breaking point.

The signs come in a variety of forms. It can be an inability to sleep, or never feeling rested despite sleeping. It can be unexplained weight gain or loss, poor memory or an inability to concentrate or remain present. In practice I see the physical presentation of this as back pain, migraine, headaches, shoulder stiffness, stomach upsets and repeated small niggly health concerns. People also become irritable, feel constantly tearful and lack patience. Some experience a combination of factors, and others a single factor, but either way these are signs and symptoms that you need to pay attention to.

Your physical non-negotiables must address:

1. **N**ourish
2. **E**xercise
3. **S**leep
4. **T**ime

Nourish

Nourishment is your physical need to eat and drink in order to function. That simple – it is about putting food and fluids into your body so that you have the energy to walk, talk, think, grow, move, smile, sleep and generally function as a human.

Diet culture has complicated our understanding of what good nourishment looks like, tricking many of us into believing that if we haven't foraged for, cooked from scratch and eaten our meals while meditating then we are not doing it right. In contrast, nourishing your body is about eating all of the food that you enjoy – including the sweets, chocolate and crisps – while making healthy choices 80 per cent of the time. It is about drinking at least two litres of water daily and limiting your intake of alcohol to ensure that you stay within public health guidelines.

In researching this book, I spoke to performance nutritionist Daniel Davey about what good nourishment really means. His advice was as practical as it was simple: eat sensible amounts based on your physical needs. Stay hydrated by drinking adequate fluids, predominantly water. There is no such thing as bad carbs, and while each of us is different, our basic nutritional needs are the same. Eat plenty of fruit and vegetables (a simple target is at least 30 different plants each week), introduce protein into each meal, and enjoy mostly slow digesting carbohydrate foods. This includes bread and, in his words, the humble spud. Have a glass of wine or beer, drink coffee and eat the odd treat, but when you do, be mindful and eat it with a mindset of enjoyment.

You don't have to forage for your food, and not everything has to be organic or home-made. With Daniel Davey's words in mind, and remembering the old adage 'Everything in moderation, including moderation itself', the notion of how to nourish your body feels more accessible and achievable.

As you begin to consider how you can better nourish yourself, grab your notebook and prepare for your Pause for 60.

Pause for 60

In these 60 seconds focus on the smallest improvements you could make in order to nourish yourself over the coming weeks.

As you do this, keep this mantra in your head: 'Think big but start small'.

These core questions act as your guide:

- What does improvement look like for you?
- What are the big things you would like to change?
- What does that really mean to you?
- What do the phases of this look like to you?
- Starting at the end and working your way backwards, what steps are involved in achieving this?
- Is there anything you have left out?
- What is the smallest thing you could do, starting today?

Be careful of 'shouldisms'

At this point, most people become a little self-critical, and have a tendency to introduce 'shouldisms'. Shouldisms are sentences of self-reproach that start with 'I should do X and Y and Z', quickly followed by asking ourselves, 'Where will I start?' and telling ourselves, 'Nobody else will do it with me and this isn't sustainable long-term.'

If this is you, please feel seen. This is a normal reaction to change, especially change that requires effort and thought. It might even feel like another 'to-do list' at the end of a long line of not-done-yet lists! Yes, life is busy and so are you, but this can be simple – really simple. You might decide to kick off by eating more fruit and vegetables. And note the use of the word 'eat' rather than 'buy'. Households in Ireland throw out an average of €700 worth of fruit and vegetable each year. If your home is anything like mine, you buy the vegetables and fruit but a large proportion never make it onto the plate! I know, we are all guilty of it.

If this sounds like your home, what is the smallest thing you could do each day to ensure that vegetables make it onto the plate? In our home we started by serving up the vegetables first – yes, you read correctly, we put one portion of vegetables on our plates at each meal time and eat them before any other food goes on the table. It took a little getting used to, but it works. We also started to put fruit out on the kitchen island at breakfast time and before we leave for school and work most of it is gone. Once that fruit starts looking a little less fresh, we make smoothies. Overall, little by little, we started to eat more fruit and vegetables without making any big significant changes.

We also bought a reusable bottle of water for each of us. The kids got a 750ml bottle in their favourite colour, and my partner and I each got a one-litre bottle. This was a simple and, more importantly, effective way to keep track of our water intake.

As you make this change, think big and act small. Ask yourself what are the small yet meaningful things that you can do to make a difference. As time moves on and this becomes a habit, ask yourself – What is the next improvement I want to make?

Exercise

Think exercise, think marathon or think gym. In fact, I was going to use the word 'movement' here instead of exercise, as I was afraid that the word 'exercise' might scare you off.

Despite coming from a family of competitive sportspeople, and taking part in sport all my life, I never really enjoyed exercise. I always associated it with competition, sweat and rain. And while I too am competitive at heart, competitive exercise just didn't turn me on. We often mistake heavy-duty, hard-core exercise that requires hours in the gym, running marathons or taking part in triathlons as the only form of 'real' exercise. The reality is that exercise is simply another word for activity.

Absolutely, it can involve training for events, taking part in competitive sport or running long distances, but that is a choice. For those who get a kick out of this it is often described as an addiction; if this rings true for you, then hold off and include this non-negotiable under personal, in the next section. But for those of us who don't fit into that category, exercise at its most simple, and in its infinitely less scary form, is about daily bodily movement. Nothing more, nothing less.

The concept of hitting 10,000 steps per day is a legacy of a marketing campaign by the first company to release a pedometer in the 1960s in Japan. This notion is founded on the belief by the company founder that the Japanese character for 10,000, *manpo-kei,* looked like a person running and his belief that the number was catchy to boot – either way he struck gold. Not only did the company sell its product, the idea of 10K steps per day as a metric for health has many of us walking around our living rooms as we watch Netflix right before we go to bed!

Is getting 10K steps a day beneficial to our health? Yes, but it is not a magic number. Research from a 2020 study with a large sample of adults over 40 during a three-year period shows that people who took between 8,000 and 12,000 daily steps were less likely to die during that time frame. Those who took 4,000 or fewer steps were more likely to die or present with mortality risk factors. Interestingly, the intensity of the steps didn't seem to matter; what was most important was movement.

So with that in mind, as you drive around the car park to get the closest space to the door – even if it's the door of the gym! – you might consider getting yourself to move a little more by parking further away. Or, if you take public transport to work, is it possible to walk one stop further from your home on your commute to and from work? Ask yourself, 'What is the smallest thing I could do today that would increase the amount of movement in my day?'

But, you may ask, is this practical? Delivering a session on this in-house with a large consultancy firm, I asked the group that very question. They were a really enthusiastic group, supported by their organisation with the structures to stay well. After the session one lady said, 'I'm going to walk home from work today and do so every day from now on.' She was both delighted and committed. But when we switched to explore the practicalities of what she had committed to, the story unfolded a little differently.

(Before you continue, I am aware that this story reinforces a stereotype, and I was tempted to change the detail to say it was a man, but I chose not to. This is the reality of how this particular event unfolded, and it shall be told as such.)

On the day in question, she was wearing high heels, and had no runners with her. Once she broke her non-negotiables into its constituent parts, she realised that walking home that evening was indeed the smallest thing she could do, but it also happened to be the least practical given her shoe situation. So instead, she committed to walking each evening starting tomorrow. If she had walked home that evening, blistered and despondent, she would have given up. But she thought big and worked it out small.

Pause for 60

In the 60 seconds that follow, focus on the smallest improvements you could make in your life to integrate more exercise into your life over the coming weeks.

As you do this, keep that mantra in your head: 'Think big but start small'.

Take the stairs more often, park away from the door of the gym or shop, get off a stop early on your commute, take movement breaks.

Activate your Permission Mindset and as you do look for small opportunities to integrate more movement into your day, week and month.

Sleep

Sleep is a hot topic, and rightly so. Arianna Huffington's 2010 TED Talk on the importance of sleep and the link adequate sleep has to success, which is titled 'How to succeed? Get More Sleep' has amassed over 5.7 million views at the time of writing. Sleep is a topic that consumes many of us, irrespective of our season of life.

As teenagers we want to go to bed late and get up late, and as young adults we want to party hard and work hard. Pulling all-nighters to get college or work projects in on time is par for the course. Those who move into parenthood wonder who came up with the saying 'sleeping like a baby', because any babies I know, in particular my own, didn't sleep like that baby, and the shock of that sleep deprivation hit hard – really hard. The hormonal change in the female body during menstruation, pregnancy and menopause requires sleep, often more of it than we can find. Recovery from illness, age and sometimes just life often requires more sleep. And sleep patterns shift and change over our lives.

Of the 168 hours available to us each week, we are meant to spend at least 56, or eight hours each night, asleep. What's more, if we can get at least two of those hours in before midnight, they are magically worth double what you get after that time – so the cliché 'early to bed and early to rise' is not simply an old wives' tale; it is grounded in science.

Lack of sleep, science tells us, profoundly impacts our ability to make decisions, to have relationships, to engage with our careers and to maintain our well-being. Science also tells us that good-quality sleep is associated with better health indicators on every single marker of well-being, including the likelihood of developing Type II diabetes or cancer, suffering heart disease, having a mental health difficulty or gaining weight.

The rules around good sleep are common sense: go to bed early, no tech in your bedroom, no TV or screen time for 30 minutes before bed. No doubt you, like me, are determined to improve your sleep routine, and yet you find yourself sitting in front of the TV binge-watching 'just one more episode'.

While not scientific in nature, over the years I have found a few simple hacks that work really well. In the evening, when you sit down to watch TV, use the sleep timer function, programming it to automatically turn off your TV 30 minutes before your chosen bedtime. To start with it feels really abrupt when the TV magically shuts down, particularly when watching an intense or funny scene. But viewed through a different lens it could also mark the start of a new routine that brings you better sleep. After the TV switches off, develop a new routine, by reading or journalling. Light a candle and make a cup of herbal tea, spend some time on your cleansing and teeth-brushing routine, rather than rushing it. Intentionally move to a routine that orients your brain towards sleep. Remember, this is not an extra 30 minutes; rather it is swapping out 30 minutes of TV to build a good sleep hygiene habit.

The blue light emitted from electronic devices, including phones, interferes with your sleep. This means that if you look around your bedroom and you can see the screen of any or all of the following – TV, tablet, phone, laptop and desktop computer – then your room is alight with blue light, and that is impacting the quality of your sleep.

Pause for 60

In the 60 seconds that follow, focus on the smallest improvements you could make in your life to integrate more sleep into your life over the coming weeks.

What is the smallest thing you could do to reduce the amount of blue light in your room? Is it possible to leave your laptop or tablet outside your bedroom door? Could you imagine leaving your phone beside it? Is there another room in your home that you could move your computer to? If not, could you cover it with something? If you need your phone for an alarm, perhaps consider buying an old-fashioned alarm clock. (Although if you, like myself, are allergic to the 'tick' of a wind-up clock, make sure to buy a battery-operated silent one.)

If you can't get your head around the idea of breaking up with your phone at night, for whatever reason, go to your phone settings and alter the screen temperature to a night setting. Activated differently on each device, the night setting changes the screen to a warmer colour and filters out some of the blue light.

As you think about this, focus on one small thing at a time. Aim for something practical and attainable.

Time

This means taking time to spend with people who make you smile. So often, in this busy world of coming, going and doing, we don't get to spend the amount of time we want with the people we love, and who love us and bring joy to our world. And too often, when we get that time, we are distracted by DMs, emails, IMs, WhatsApp or the like.

After we had our first baby my partner took time off to be with us when we were in hospital. At the time there was no paternity leave, and he had just started his own business, so the amount of time that he could take off was limited. When we came home from hospital, he went to work the following day. He didn't want to go. I didn't want him to go. He was working with a number of businesses, and one of them pressured him to attend a meeting. He wanted to keep the contract, and as it was a new business he was anxious that things worked out. He went. That was 11 years ago now, and to this day he still regrets going. By choice, he no longer contracts into that business. Hindsight is 20/20, and he is now in a stronger position of agency, but where and how we spend our time is important.

A C-suite dad of four I recently interviewed, named Tom, told me that he leaves work every single day at 5 p.m., never does meetings before 10 a.m., and drops his kids to school three days a week. He admits that this wasn't always easy, but he was adamant that he was not going to be the corporate dad that his own father was. He also shared with me that, when he moved to his current position, he had itchy feet for a while, but he was clear about the type of role he wanted during this season of his life. As his children were growing up he applied only for roles in organisations that had Dublin-based global HQs. Tom clarified that this meant travel was typically into Dublin rather than out of Dublin to a HQ elsewhere in the world. He admits that some of these choices have meant that he has not moved to the bigger pay cheque at the next stage, but he believes the rewards outweigh any such losses.

Orla, a friend of mine leading the financial function of a tech business, only travels once per month when required to do so, and must always be home on weekends. She is heavily involved as a volunteer with a charity, and has a strong core group of friends who she enjoys spending time with. She also has some hens, ducks and a dog who she doesn't want to be away from.

In each of their shapes and forms, the decisions made by Tom and Orla are based on spending time with people who make them smile. Sure, we could suggest that their hierarchical position allows them to do this, but when I put that question to Orla, she replied candidly, 'You know, I have a boss as well.' The point is that, no matter the season of your life or your hierarchical position, there is always someone looking for more of you, and there comes a point where you have to make the decision: your needs or their needs.

As you consider this in the context of your life, and your needs, what are your non-negotiables? Who are the people who make you smile? Do you spend quality time with them? Do you have the opportunity to do so? Is it possible to have one night per week without TV or devices in order to chat to each other? Could you meet for coffee or lunch weekly? Ask yourself, what is the smallest thing you could do to increase the amount of quality time you spend with people who make you smile.

As a parent of four small children I find this really hard. When I scroll social media it appears as though so many people have this figured out. But in reality I have friends I haven't seen in months, and two of them live across the road! During lockdown two of my dearest friends, Laura and Helen, and I started a virtual book club that met a sum total of never. My husband and I never do date night because by the time we have a babysitter organised, get the kids to bed, get dressed up and head off, frankly it's time to go to bed. So I get that this is really bloody hard.

The compromise is that my husband and I meet for coffee

in our local coffee shop once a week. We also don't watch TV on Thursday evening; instead we cook a nice meal and have a drink together. We use that time to catch up with each other and plan for the following week. Sometimes we just sit in silence – that silence we noticed in other couples when we were younger and hoped we'd never be like them. Now we *are* them, and now we know that many of them were happily sitting in silence, listening only to the ringing in their ears after the noise of the day had subsided!

Most of my friends and I visit each other twice a year and attempt an odd call in between. I go for dinner with my friends who live a stone's throw away, twice a year or so. The rest of the time we have half conversations at school gates, around pick-ups or drop-offs or when our children are entertaining each other for a while. My family and I have chats on the phone, exchange voice notes or have dinner together to celebrate special occasions.

For now, during this season of our lives, that is enough. It's not perfect, but it's enough, and when it happens it makes us all smile.

Pause for 60

In this Pause for 60 focus on how you can make time to take time with people who make you smile. As you do, keep in mind the opening story of this chapter. Are you including yourself as someone worthy of spending time with?

What comes to mind for you? Remember to break the rules of what you *think* you should or should not do. What do you want to do? Who do you want to spend time with? Who makes you smile? Based on all of that information, what's your plan?

Personal non-negotiables

Your personal non-negotiables are the core things you need in place in order to live a happy and content life. They are unique to you, so while there are guidelines to follow, there are no absolutes attached. So what are your personal non-negotiables, and why are they important?

Your personal non-negotiables are linked to the things that support you in your lifestyle choices. They are the activities, hobbies and interests that provide you with a sense of happiness and calmness, and the finances that you need to support these activities. They may not make sense to others, but that really doesn't matter. The important thing is that you understand their centrality to your life, how they contribute to your enjoyment of life and how they connect you to yourself and others.

Money

But first the finances. No matter what anybody says, money matters. You need to understand how much money you need to earn to pay for the important things in life. For example, what are your monthly financial needs for food, rent/mortgage, crèche, health and utility bills, dog kennels, health insurance, transport, etc.? There is nothing more stressful than struggling to pay your basic bills.

My Granny Brady told me to 'Make no man your God and always have your own money.' It was simple but sage advice, from the mouth of a woman who had had to leave a permanent, pensionable job as a psychiatric nurse because she got married. She left home at 16 and went to the north of Ireland, where she trained, becoming the first Catholic ward sister of her time. When she met my grandfather and they decided to get married she had to leave that job not because she wanted to, but because it was her legal duty to do so. At the time, the marriage bar meant that upon marriage women had to leave their job to attend to their duties within the home. She offered this advice earnestly, because she knew the impact that this law had had on generations of women.

So this advice is here, and it is aimed at women specifically, with one caveat addressed later, because we know that the purse strings in homes, even where both partners are in paid employment, tend to be controlled by male partners. While the completeness of this control has shifted in the past 25 years, the hangover remains. Women tend not to have a pension plan, savings or access to money for a rainy day. Research also shows that a small minority of men, but nonetheless significant in terms of numbers, are in relationships where they are financially controlled, allowed only access to a weekly allowance or when granted it by their partner.

Financial control, whatever form it takes, is domestic abuse, and where it exists, on its own or in tandem with other forms of abuse, for either men or women, it is wrong. If you find yourself in this position, reach out and ask for help, be it through the employee assistance programme in your workplace or by speaking to someone in the Samaritans or St Vincent de Paul.

In terms of your career, knowing your financial health puts you in a position of agency over any decisions that you may make about staying or going. When making the decision to leave my permanent, pensionable job, my partner and I sat with a spreadsheet and highlighted every single incoming and outgoing. His attention to detail in all things finances is heartbreakingly brilliant and frustrating. It caused tears and tantrums, for both of us.

Using a traffic light system, we figured out exactly how much we needed to survive, what we could do without and what we could spend a little on. The figures highlighted in red included our mortgage, health insurance, car insurance, loans and childcare, as well as utility and food bills. Those in amber were things we could do without but if we had 'leftover' money we could splurge on. This included essential new clothes, dinner out, hairdressers (I wasn't blonde at the time) and other small things, like the fancy cheese and wine that we love. Green was for out-of-the-question items, which meant no holidays or weekends away. We cancelled our TV subscriptions and ruled out other discretionary purchases.

Adding the red figures together meant we knew the basic income we needed to take in every month. That in turn allowed us to break it down into a weekly and hourly rate, so when we went to our paid work, we knew to the hour how much we needed to earn. Despite the challenge of doing this, it was worthwhile, and things suddenly seemed less scary, as we needed less money to manage than we first thought. Much of what we considered essential was in fact discretionary spends. And looking back over Covid, many of us realised that we could do with less of the things we once considered essential.

If you are thinking about developing in your career, and if this is going to require time out of the paid workforce, budgeting of this sort is a must-do exercise, as it gives you the raw financial data you need in order to decide whether you have the leeway to leave your paid job before finding a new role.

A core part of your personal non-negotiables is knowing and understanding how much money you have, how much you need, how much you can spend, and how much you can save. Despite how simple it sounds on paper, doing it is not an easy or relished task. From the bottom of my heart, it is one I hate. I don't know why, but I fear the figures and worry that I will never have enough, but I don't even know how much is enough.

Based on working with thousands of clients over the past 10 years, this is the Achilles heel of many. Accounting, planning or managing finances is something that for some reason I have a fear of.

Pause for 60

In this Pause for 60 your entire focus is on knowing your financial basics. Having this information changes your relationship with money, bringing into focus a more mindful and conscious approach to spending on what you need rather than what you want. It also speaks to the quest for a sustainable career, in that what you do today does not prevent you from doing what you need in the future.

This will 100 per cent take more than 60 seconds to figure out, but at this moment in this space you are acknowledging the need to understand your finances and in so doing make a plan for how you are going to do so.

After taking care of your finances, your personal non-negotiables become a little more fun, if I dare say that.

Work patterns and flexibility

Closely related to finance and a factor that impacts your financial outgoings is your access to work patterns and flexibility. Traditional work patterns demanded a specific location, with default start and end times. For years, we cried out for more flexibility and the opportunity to work at times and places of our choosing.

Covid-19 government-mandated lockdowns showed us that flexible work patterns, including working from home (WFH), or indeed working from anywhere (WFA) works, and that we can make it work. Yes, it has its drawbacks, there are teething problems, but we must remember that many of those drawbacks of these work patterns were associated with stay-at-home mandates, not with WFH or WFA per se.

Globally, workers are saying that they want to retain flexibility. This does not mean that either working in an office is right or that working from home is right; it simply means that flexibility must be an option.

Pause for 60

So with your Permission Mindset activated, Pause for 60 and focus on the type of work pattern that works for you during this season of your life. In short, what are your work pattern non-negotiables?

- Do you want to WFA, follow a hybrid model, or return to the office?
- What are your needs and how much travel are you willing to do for your job?
- Do you want to work internationally and travel accordingly?
- Would you prefer to live in the countryside or a smaller urban centre, commuting to work two days per week?
- Or do you want to return to the office full-time?
- Are you unsure and really don't know (yet)?

As you reflect on your work pattern non-negotiables, remember there is no right or wrong answer here, there is only your answer.

Focus on what works for you during this season of your life, and why.

Spirituality

Spirituality for some people forms an integral part of their personal non-negotiables. A highly accomplished CEO I met recently spoke at length about her deep faith and the central role it plays in her life. I was very taken by how this for her was an unwavering need. While there was no suggestion in a single word that she spoke that I should share her faith, she was clear, Mass multiple times per week and each Saturday and Sunday was essential for her.

Another close friend practises meditation every day. It is a vital part of her life, and an absolute personal non-negotiable. Without it she feels unsettled and ungrounded, and it helps her to cope with any issues that arise in her life, inside work or otherwise.

Spirituality comes in a variety of shapes and forms; it is not a one-size-fits-all solution, but if it is integral to your life, or if you would like it to be, include the time to practise it into your personal non-negotiables.

Pause for 60

During this Pause for 60 focus on what is important to you from a spiritual perspective. Activating your Permission Mindset, afford yourself the opportunity to understand what role, if any, spirituality plays in your life.

Relieve yourself of the 'shouldisms' we spoke about earlier and instead choose what you personally want.

Hobbies and interests

Little-known fact, but a hugely important one: the word 'hobby' is derived from the Latin for recreation, which literally means to *re-create* yourself through activities done for the sole purpose of enjoyment. Hobbies and interests are not a luxury. They are a central activity core to your enjoyment of life.

Be it culture, art, sport, interiors, reading or anything else that you do in your leisure or discretionary time, their benefits include improved well-being, as well as a heightened sense of connection to self and with others. It doesn't matter if you pursue your recreational activities alone, as part of a group or through a mix of both, the ultimate outcome is a sense of physical, emotional and psychological re-creation.

As life gets busy our time gets lost doing all of the 'things', and we forget the things that make us happy, and bring us joy.

Pause for 60

The focus of this Pause for 60 is to get you thinking about what it is that you do for fun – for nothing else but for fun. The things that make you laugh, bring you comfort and, after having done them (even if you didn't want to in the first place), you always feel the better for getting up and doing it.

Use the following questions to guide your thinking:

- If you were free to do whatever you wanted, what would it be?
- What are you most drawn to do?

- What hobbies and interests did you enjoy as a child? Do you still enjoy these activities, or do you have new ones? Either way, do you feel you have the time to include them in life?
- What activities make you feel healthier, happier, more content, less frustrated and more engaged?

A typical answer to one of these questions might be, 'I really used to love yoga, but over the past few years I just got out of the habit, and if I'm honest I feel guilty if I take the time to do it.'

Remember, your personal non-negotiables support you in your endeavour to thrive, flourish and progress in life, in work and in your career. So with that in mind, activate your Permission Mindset and ask yourself, 'What is the smallest thing I can do to improve my personal non-negotiables?'

Professional non-negotiables

Last but certainly not least are your professional non-negotiables. While typically put before your physical and personal non-negotiables, the home of your professional non-negotiables, even if it feels counter-intuitive, is in third position. This does not reflect the importance of your professional non-negotiables; rather it speaks to the fact that failure to consider your physical and personal well-being will result in an out-of-sync feeling, one in which you never feel fully accomplished or satisfied, even when in acceleration mode.

Your professional non-negotiables are the parts of your role that are necessary for you to feel sustained and engaged in your work. Some professional non-negotiables align with your values, while others align with the functional aspects of your role. It is a combination of what you do and the purpose for which you do it that is important.

For some people, working in a socially meaningful role in the not-for-profit sector is important. This type of work is what we refer to as cause-related work, and knowing that this is a professional non-negotiable helps you to determine the sector you want to work in. In terms of sector, you might focus your attention on government, public or private, technology or the start-up community.

This in turn helps you to clarify if you need or want job permanency or security. Perhaps you can spend time in a role that lacks these certainties but offers access to other opportunities you might not otherwise get. This might involve exposure to new technology, or a new system that you see future value in.

In practice, I find that many who leave roles do so due to lack of career progression opportunities, which is often associated with the size or structure of their current organisation. If this is the case, one of your professional non-negotiables may be to work in a larger organisation with structured in-house career development programmes that provide access to mentoring and sponsorship.

Positive workplace culture is another that finds its way onto many non-negotiable lists. While important, figuring this out is like solving a riddle. What is a positive culture, and how do you know if an organisation has one? While culture is something you feel rather than define, there are a few key indicators you can watch out for.

For example, an organisation with a low turnover rate and a high incidence of referrals for roles are good starting points. Low turnover rates typically mean that people stay because it is a good place to work, and if those staff refer others, including their friends, to work in that organisation, that speaks volumes.

Another indicator of fairness and transparency is an organisation's gender pay gap. If it is lower than average and there are efforts to close it year on year the likelihood is that the organisation values fairness and transparency. Checking out Glassdoor and other rating sites can help, but ultimately, talking to people within the organisation and asking them what their experience is is the path to greatest knowledge.

For others, a people-facing role in a busy environment that involves working as part of a team is central. And yet another person may value the same role but need the opportunity to work on projects independently. The opportunity to access organisation-funded learning and development may be significant for you, or having the chance to hone your language skills. Perhaps it is important to you to have autonomy and control over your workload, or maybe you are happy to defer to a more senior person.

The list is endless, and it is unique to you. It depends on the stage you are at in your career, and what you want next. The key is that you have a core set of professional non-negotiables that are meaningful and important to you. They may reflect, or not, some of the above recommendations. You may have other professional non-negotiables that are relevant to the season of life that you are in.

Jen's story

Jen, a client in her mid-30s, was moving role before Covid, and one of her professional non-negotiables was to find a role in an organisation that would support her journey to parenthood. Currently single, she wanted to work for an organisation that had robust leave options that supported the multiple pathways to parenthood under consideration for her. This included surrogacy, adoption, egg freezing, IVF and maternity leave when the time came. She did not want to be the first in her organisation to travel this path, as she felt that manoeuvring through all of that red tape alongside a lack of family support would be too much.

Coming from a very traditional family, the idea of conceiving a child through fertility treatment and outside a stable heterosexual marriage was considered shameful. Her parents had already shared their thoughts and made it clear that she would not have their support. Having an organisation and friends to support her was important to her during this season of her life. Therefore, companies with supportive practices and policies in place were professional non-negotiables for Jen.

Pause for 60

As you begin to think about your professional non-negotiables, what triggers you?

Is it about company or organisation size? Is their culture important to you? What are your values, and how important is it that they align with certain industries, job types or organisations? Is it important for you to have access to career development and growth opportunities? What about mentoring and sponsorship? Do you want to work as part of a team, independently or a mix of both?

These are important questions to understand and have an answer to. Knowing them puts you in a position of choice and agency over your decision-making process, and if you need to compromise at least you do so in the full knowledge of why you are making that decision. Based on this, you can rationalise the decision for yourself, and instead of it feeling like an unexplained sacrifice, it is a choice that you made for several reasons that are important and significant to you.

Remember, your physical non-negotiables are required for survival, and your personal non-negotiables support you in your endeavour to thrive, flourish and progress in life, in work and in your career.

One piece of paper

Once you have figured out your non-negotiables, take a piece of paper and under each heading – Physical, Personal and Professional – record your decisions. Make it clear and simple and keep the words to as few as possible. As you move forward in crafting your sustainable career, these words protect your nos and preserve your yeses.

PART THREE

Success: The Power to Design Your Own Version

CHAPTER 9
Design Your Own Success

Living in the grey

A sustainable career represents a leap to freedom, a freedom born out of understanding that sweet spot where life, work and career happen side by side, a space and a place within which it is possible to thrive, progress and flourish in life *and* your career. Comfort lies in the fact that you understand, and have given yourself permission to access the deeply interconnected nature of life, work and career, and how each is tethered to your current season of life.

Naming jobs, or suggesting a career, or binding you to an industry could be counterproductive as you continuously re-evaluate, recontract and renegotiate your relationship with the world of work and the new and interesting roles that appear almost daily.

As you consider this, remind yourself that it is completely reasonable *not to know* exactly what it is that you plan to do with your life. We all need a 'vocational myth detox', a conscious and deliberate purge of a long-held belief that has gnawed away at our legitimate hopes, one that has led you on a pathway that may no longer serve you, and perhaps never did.

Although finding it is an immense challenge that should not be underestimated, it is also one that, with time and energy, it is possible to do. As we discovered, however, this skill is seldom taught in an education system that expects complete answers to complicated problems, or where rote learning is demanded. This is the fault not of educators but of a curriculum designed to feed a neoliberalist logic in which creativity, criticism and challenge are allowed, but only as long as they preserve the status quo.

Our minds struggle to sort scattered information into a coherent body of thought unless we train them to do so. This involves grappling with questions that feel uncomfortable. It is finding peace with our natural human tendency to shy away from anything that feels daunting.

But within you lies the ability to sift through this information. It is through this process that the data emerges and you begin to understand what it is that you desire during specific seasons of your life. It is the collective power of career stories of our time that shift the narrative, through which you will have a more sustainable career and pave the path for the generations that follow.

This is your chance to write the story of your future sustainable career, by you and for you. This is your opportunity to commit to paper your next step, your next choice and your next chapter. In it you are invited to design your own version of success, using all the information you have gathered on your journey so far.

Remember, understanding your career journey requires you to plan, think, construct, deconstruct and reconstruct. The confusion that this represents is not a failing on your part to find a calling or vocation; rather it is a normal reaction to peeling back the layers of influence that have built up over the years. That confusion is a normal sensation presented as feedback between your body and brain as you start to think differently and adopt the position of a career critic.

Acknowledge your confusion, and name it as a signal that your career is deeply important to you. If you did not care about your career, you would not feel that confusion, or the irritation caused by that confusion.

This is the exciting part, the piece of the puzzle in which you get to think about the future on your terms, armed with the knowledge that the previous decisions, those made in a sociocultural context that remained unquestioned for generations, were not really your own. That context meant you made decisions about your career and your future based on someone else's story.

We recalled the history of this in the early chapters, and critically considered the cultural rules we are accustomed to. We spoke about how these codes help us to navigate a complex world. This, we know, is sometimes helpful, especially when explicitly stated; for example, knowing that red is the universal traffic light colour for stop takes the guessing out of what to do as you travel through new lands.

On the other hand, the implicit rules, the silent ones, that tell you how to earn the approval of others if you want to be accepted, are often not that helpful. It is the striving to operate within those rules that may have led you to read this book in the first place, rules designed in the 1900s, reinforced in the 1950s and applied to a workplace that is of a different decade or generation, of a different millennium, one that is now unrecognisable.

Five, 10, 15 or 20 years ago, you did not have access to the set of diverse jobs and careers in industries that you do today. Now, there are new jobs, careers and industries waiting for you, opportunities ranging from solo employment, to short-term consultancy contracts, to working as a contractor; the world, with all of its gloriously frustrating idiosyncrasies, is your oyster.

Time travel

To do this, you will time travel (remember your autobiographical memory) within and between the pages of this book to recall, revisit and refine the information you have gathered so far. As you grow into your role as author of your future career, you will learn to cast a critical eye on the opportunities and next steps and to think about success on your terms. As you do, you will build an exit strategy, one that paves the way to your next step, or one that you trigger when you are in a position of struggle or unhappiness. Each of these components is important, and together they form a set of skills that you can refine over time.

I worked with a client some years ago who came to me distraught and upset. A life coach had advised her to resign from her job to spend time manifesting her ideal job. Her life coach had assured her that this would work, and that within three months she would find herself in her ideal role. This young lady, who was very vulnerable at the time, and in need of specialised counselling to recover from an early childhood trauma, found herself unemployed, without a job or income and in a particularly tenuous situation. While well-intentioned, this life coach was not properly trained or skilled, and did not hold membership of any professional body.

So if you choose to share your experience with someone, ensure that person is an adequately qualified professional. And with that in mind, if you are following this book without the support of a professionally qualified coach, mentor or support network, I implore you to find support before making major life-changing decisions. If you choose not to, please do not leave a job until you are in the financial position to do so.

If your mental health is suffering due to the role you are in, leave if you must, but before you do so find a way to work so that you can pay your bills. That might mean agency or temporary work, or working in an industry you wouldn't normally choose, but protecting your health is vital.

What about success?

As you navigate this section, you are going to think a lot about success, a term that is often thrown around, and typically is defined through the eyes of another. We each know the success stories, the famous ones and the not-so-famous ones from the friend of a friend. Success is this beautiful state, a fairy tale that we all reach for, but it is built on the myths we deconstructed in Part One.

It goes something like this: From the moment she started school she knew exactly what she wanted to do. She excelled in relevant subjects and went to university on a scholarship. An all-rounder, she played sport for her country and by the time she finished university she had built a scalable business that was ready for venture funding. She wasn't sure if this is what she wanted, so she entered a corporate graduate programme as a back-up. Swinging from one branch of success to the next, she passed her professional exams and was ready for career progression. At the time her side hustle was doing well, so she left her job and invested in her business. Working hard, she went through three rounds of venture funding and floated her business on the New York Stock Exchange before she was 40. Always there for her children and family, she managed to have it all. She retired aged 50 and for the remainder of her life she worked on personally meaningful projects. She died peacefully in her holiday home in France, aged 93, surrounded by her equally successful family and friends.

I know this story and you know this story, but this is the story that 0.01 per cent of the world live. Her story is admirable and incredible, but also 100 per cent fictional. It is a dream, a life lived through the lens of complete success with no failure of note either personally or professionally. And while it may sound gorgeous, and a younger version of me would have completely bought into this dream, my older self understands that without experiencing the range of emotions, the trials and tribulations of life, you exist in a state of numbness in which you are unable to experience life. This dream is an inauthentic one that we all too often compare our lived reality to, and as a result we manage to find fault with each and every action we take.

Have you heard of Cathal Gaffney? Cathal, with his friend Darragh O'Connell, founded Brown Bag Films in 1994. For his work as an animator he was twice nominated for an Academy Award, once in 2000 and again in 2010. Brown Bag is responsible for some pretty incredible cartoons, including *Doc McStuffins, Eureka!* and *Ada Twist, Scientist*. The 1,100-strong workforce create a diverse and innovative supply of cartoons for some of the largest streaming platforms in the world, including Disney and Netflix. In 2015, Brown Bag Films was acquired by Story 9, making Cathal a very wealthy man.

But did you know that Cathal got kicked out of animation school? Or that when he was nominated for his first Academy Award he couldn't afford the plane ticket to the ceremony? That is not a rags to riches story. But it is the truth. Cathal, a clever creative at heart, struggled in school. To cope with having to go to school, he would go out to his garden shed to draw. Based on this interest he decided to go to college to study animation. But he got kicked out of college in his third year because he refused to do animation the way the college wanted him to. His type of animation was new, and he believed in it. Working out of that same shed, with a friend he continued to do his type of animation. While he suffered multiple rejections and failures, had no money and, in his own words, his parents were ready to give up on him, he kept going, and it worked out for him.[1]

But Cathal's success story is real, and the flip side of that showreel reveals the reality of success and the hardships endured to achieve it. We don't often hear that part, but we always hear about the success. So as you move forward with writing your sustainable career story, it is essential that you consider what success looks like for you – real success, and not success defined through comparison.

Put simply, you are going to design success by you and for you. This doesn't mean that you shouldn't consider the opinion of others or look to others for inspiration. Instead, it means that before you look to others, or consider their opinion, you are going to figure out what success means to you during this season of your life.

The aim is to understand the parameters of importance in your life, to consider how those parameters intersect with life, work and career, and to arrive at a personalised definition of success that is meaningful to you and those you share your life with.

As you think back over your life, work and career, how has your definition of success changed? Do you define success today on the same terms as you did 10, 15 or 20 years ago? Is your definition of success today the same as it was pre-Covid? At first glance these questions are simple, yet if you take a deep dive the answers reveal themselves as complex and multifaceted. Everyone wants to be happy and successful, yet by some cruel modern paradox it is the pursuit of both that often is the very reason we are unhappy!

Understandably, we each yearn to be the best version of ourselves – great professionals, the best parents, strong partners, good friends, healthy, fit and social (both online and offline). Yet the speed at which we must travel through life to achieve this often leaves us stressed, drained and overstretched. The expectation and unquestioning belief that happiness and success should look a certain way doesn't always make us feel good. The associated culture of perfection means that the juggle to achieve success becomes more of an act of torture than one filled with possibility.

Success lives in the grey

So let's start off with the basics. There is no single definition of success. Nor is there a uniform, cookie-cutter way to perform success during any season of life. Yet we so often go about achieving it according to the standards and ideals set by someone else. No one is 100 per cent successful or happy all the time. Success is a strange phenomenon, a subjective, internal feeling measured objectively.

And although the way we think about, define and go about achieving success differs radically from person to person, we each tend to follow universal steps in our pursuit of it. To do this we often turn our attention to friends, family, peers, work colleagues, admired business leaders or influencers. With this evolves a standardised age and stage notion of how to perform success. And success defined on these terms works for very few.

It is predicated upon the notion that everyone is neuro-typical, able-bodied, heterosexual, cis-gender, with children and working in a professional career, the aim of which is to pay a mortgage, buy a car and go on holidays. This type of success is often associated with a ruthless dedication to work, and to achieving more and more until you scale the highest heights of the ladder of life and your career.

To be clear, there is nothing wrong with this approach in and of itself, but we must acknowledge the facts, that prescriptive and restrictive narratives focused on outer indicators of success visible to others failed many generations who did not fit within the parameters of this definition of success, either partially or completely. Trying to simply copy someone else's formula didn't work then, and it doesn't work now.

If you want to define your own version of success, you

must take a deep dive inside yourself, as success can only be defined for you, by you. Sure, take hints from important people in your life – it's a good idea to borrow from best practices – but to craft a sustainable career, one in which you thrive, flourish and progress in life *and* your career, now and in the future, you are searching for something more nuanced and introspective. To do this you are going to peel back the deep layers of influence that have taught you to think, act and perform your life and career in a certain way.

As you begin to listen to yourself, and as the process of acknowledging what the most comfortable version of success is for you during this season of your life, it is remarkable the choices that you make. Those choices may be big and scary or small and manageable or sit on the spectrum of choices that exist between these binaries. Whatever that version of success looks like, make sure it is yours.

Pause for 60

During this Pause for 60 you are focused on outlining what success looks like for you during this season of life. Activate your Permission Mindset and freely consider what success designed by you, for you means to you during this season of your life.

To do this you rely on the information you have built across the course of this book. Bring yourself back to the seasons of life and using your physical, personal and professional non-negotiables as a guide, consider what success, real meaningful success, is to you during this season of your life.

For the remainder of this book, you are invited to think about that version of success in the context of three different versions of a sustainable career. As you do, you are asked to Pause for 60, and to think, reflect and problem-solve. In these moments of pause, you will identify connections, patterns and lacunae between where you currently are and where you want to go.

In doing so you present yourself with a variety of possible future selves with which you begin to plan your next steps in a way that respects the point at which life, work and career intersect during this season of your life. It is a new and different way of thinking about your career, but it presents a sustainable one that you can live and work in at the same time.

The next practical step

As you progress through this phase of thinking about your future sustainable career, work your way through a series of questions, beginning with: What would you do next if you did what is expected of you? In other words, what is the next logical step in your career?

As you do so, activate your Permission Mindset. Take the time to purposefully write it down and explore what it would look like. Admittedly, this is not the most exciting of questions, but it a very important one. Its purpose is to prompt you to think about your future career identity in your current role, and to consider how you feel about the prospect of that future.

You might remember the story about my decision to leave a permanent, pensionable job, which at the time was a tough decision. When I was faced with this exact question, and when I put pen to paper about my next logical step, my future career felt dark; it felt like one that would likely be stagnant, with little opportunity to grow, explore or develop because of my environment. As the words found my page, tears welled up in my eyes, and a big lump formed in my throat. My reaction was visceral. I knew I had to go, but it took several years to make that decision final.

Comparing that to how I feel about my future career now, there is no comparison. The next logical step is one full of possibility and excitement. It's not 100 per cent perfect, and there are worries about financial stability and the scalability of the business, but these challenges feel manageable. In five years' time, that may have changed, but for now the next logical step in my career is the one I want.

So as you engage with this activity, don't feel compelled to undervalue the next logical step because you think you should, or might like to do something different, in the future. Hold the possibility that perhaps your next logical step may be the right one, during this season of your life. As you delve a little deeper, consider what career progression looks like from within your organisation or industry.

Pause for 60

This Pause for 60 focuses on the next practical step. Doing so helps you to figure out if this possible future appeals to you. If so, why? If not, why not? Is your next practical step open to you within your current role, organisation and industry? If so, what evidence do you have of this? If not, what evidence do you have to contradict this? What is it about this next logical step that appeals to you? What is it about this next logical step that doesn't appeal to you? Are there parts of this story that look exciting for you? Are there any parts that look bleak to you?

Remember, there are few jobs or roles, even the ones that you really don't enjoy, that in totality are bleak or lacking in excitement. There are always parts you like and parts you dislike.

As you do this activity, take the opportunity to listen to both sides of your story and how you truly feel about the next logical step. Include information about the parts you like and dislike. At this point, check in with yourself, notice if you are writing about more likes or dislikes. In practice, depending on how you feel about your next logical step, you may, subconsciously, focus on either your likes or your dislikes. Overt focus on either raises the possibility of a poorly informed decision, or the failure to fully consider each of your options.

If you choose to take, or not, your next logical step, it is important that you know your 'why', as this information informs whatever decision you make. When you took your unfiltered snapshot of your career in Chapter 6 and, as you defined success in this chapter, you considered the decisions and factors that got you to this point in your career.

Peeling back the layers of influence, you worked hard to figure out vital information about how you got to this point in your career. Now is the time to use that information as you move forward.

If you take the next logical step in your career, how much agency and control are you likely to have over how you write the story of your career? Does this feel sustainable for you? If so, why? If not, why not? What definition of success did you follow until now? Who and what informed that definition? Does that definition of success still serve you? What would success look like for you if you followed the next logical step?

Admittedly there are many more questions than answers, but like the fable of the hare and the tortoise, slow and steady wins the race.

Job crafting

Job crafting involves taking positive, proactive steps to re-design the work that you do. When done well, you are supported by your team and organisation. In fact, emerging research shows that collective job crafting at an organisational level within and between teams shows great promise for increasing engagement, meaning and enjoyment at work. The premise of job crafting is simple: stay in your existing role but proactively manage tasks or aspects of your role that are within your control.[2]

The easiest way to job craft is to ask yourself, 'What is the smallest thing I can do to personalise my job/role so that it works better for me?' Job crafting is a particularly useful technique if you must stay in a job, career or industry that you don't like, meaning you must bide your time until you can transition into something else. Job crafting looks different for everyone, and the form that it takes depends on your season of life and your career phase and what impact you desire.

For example, if you are in the season of life where you just need to get your job done with ease and little pressure, to clock in and clock out on time, and your focus is to earn money, then job crafting looks different for you than for someone in full career progression mode, and who has time, money and energy to invest in that progression.

In the first instance, you may choose to craft your job through collaboration. This might involve talking to other team members, colleagues in different departments or in other organisations to see if there is a different way of approaching a task, overcoming a challenge or coming up with an innovation. In the second instance, you might decide to put your hand up for a stretch opportunity – you need a challenge, so you will either choose to get involved in a new project or create the opportunity to work in something that interests you.

If, on the other hand, you are considering moving role, job or industry and you need to better understand what that change might look like, you may decide to craft your role, where possible, to gain exposure to the skills that you may need going forward. This requires a shift in mindset, and for you to think broadly and without rules. This allows you through a lens of curiosity to get the opportunity you want.

Pause for 60

In this Pause for 60, focus on visualising yourself living and working in your next logical step. What is your role and what type of identity do you assume? How do you feel? Who are your colleagues and co-workers? What have you achieved? Who are the important people in your life? How do you manage your non-negotiables?

As you play around with a variety of possible future career stories you may notice a shift in how you experience your identity. Once again, listen to this feedback and use it to help you make your next step.

At the end of this exercise, you may decide that you are taking your next logical step. Or you may decide that you are happy for now. Whatever your decision, factor in review time each week, month and year to see how you are going and if you are still content with your decision.

Remember, nothing is forever, and that is the essence of a sustainable career, the ongoing ability to review and think.

A challenging step

Now we shift the tempo, and you are tasked with taking a challenging next step. This is a career or work-related step that stretches you, and should you decide to take it, most likely it requires an investment of your time, energy and expertise. It may require a financial element, geographical change or a shift in some of your non-negotiables, but you should keep this in mind when making your final decision.

As you write about your challenging step you will feel stretched, pushed and extended but also excited and uplifted. That doesn't mean that you must commit all of you to this step; rather, it is the start of a different career story, a more sustainable one for you. It is a choice to push forward, to press play and to progress or pause in your career. You are playing with the options open to you, that possibility that is within reach, but requires effort and forward momentum to achieve.

Challenge will come in many different shapes and forms, so just as with success, your definition of what is challenging really matters! You must think about the definition of a challenging step from your own unique and personal perspective.

Pause for 60

As you Pause for 60, activate your Permission Mindset and with freedom write what a challenging career step might look like for you. Depending on the season of life that you are living in and your experience of that season, to build a sustainable career you are going to make choices that make your life a better one, both now and in the future.

A challenging step could be to take things more slowly, to press pause, and to live life while earning a living. For some a challenging step is changing organisation, particularly if you have worked in the same organisation for your entire career or for a number of years. The idea of facing interviews, meeting new colleagues, a different commute or a change in office environment is your definition of a challenge. It may be the decision to press eject from your current role, to pursue a different career in a new industry, or it might be to stay within your current industry and shift roles. Shifting industry, role or organisation may require you to upskill, reskill or retrain. Choosing to shift gears to do this for others is a challenging step.

So how do you know what your next challenging step is? Well, that's a good question. To achieve this you must enter explore mode.

Entering explore mode

Entering explore mode means that you promise to activate your Permission Mindset with the clear intention of remaining curious and asking questions (lots of questions).

Pause for 60

Based on what you have just written about a challenging step, go into the detail a little deeper. Pause for 60 and ask:

'What if there were no rules?'

'What if I tried?'

'What if I could?'

'What would I do then?'

'What then? And what next?'

Remember, as you enter explore mode you are exploring on paper only. Don't confuse exploration with decision-making time or commitment. Yes, we are taught that once we write something down it turns into a goal, and that goal then turns into a plan. And while there is an element of truth to that, the extent of that truth is something else altogether. Yes, writing something down is helpful; it powers your brain up to think in a different way, but it does not move you from thought to action, nor does it commit you to *do* what you have written down.

If you formulate a plan with strategic actions and then move to put those actions in place you are goal-striving – that is altogether different. At this point, you are designing your own version of success, a sustainable type of success, with the express aim of exploring a challenging move in your career, nothing more, nothing less.

You are considering the idea and the potential in multiple options. As such, you are a distance from making any decision, let alone *the* decision. With that in mind, shift back into explore mode.

Multiple challenges

As you enter into this more creative space, one that opens up previously discarded or disregarded areas, you may open a Pandora's box of challenging next steps to explore. If this is the case, I recommend that you brainstorm each of the challenging next steps one at a time. Remember, this is not about making a clear and definitive decision; it's about putting *all* possibilities on paper – and let's face it, what is the worst that could happen if you write something down?

Pause for 60

Activate your Permission Mindset, and as you do, permit yourself to write down each of the challenging next steps. Titles, courses, jobs, whatever comes into your head, allow it to live on paper. Give each option a blank sheet of paper. Over the course of a single session, begin to explore each of your challenging options.

Stick to one at a time and really focus on the content. Be both descriptive and prescriptive as you do this.

You are playing with a variety of possible future career identities as you do this activity. As you write, step into character, visualise yourself doing that next challenging step. Think about: What *exactly* is the challenge involved if I were to choose this step?

Nature begins to play tricks on you at this point, and if it is, you will notice that you are writing down words for the sake of writing down words, or you are using buzzwords to describe what you are thinking. For example, if you find words or phrases like 'It will be hard', or 'I am not sure', then nature is taking over, and you are using empty signifiers to cloud your judgement.

Empty vessels make the most noise

Just as empty vessels make the most noise, so too do empty signifiers. An empty signifier, in psychological speak, refers to words or phrases that we all use to describe something or indeed everything, but we really don't know what they mean to us, or to others. Take the 'It will be hard' example above. What do you really mean by 'hard'? Do you think it will require too much effort? Are you happy to try, or is too hard really a deal-breaker for you?

What about 'I'm not sure?' Are you unsure because you haven't done enough research? Or is it because you have so much information that you are in overwhelm mode and can't decide? Or is it 'I'm not sure' because you don't think you can do it, or because you don't have the confidence?

And on that note of confidence – confidence is one of those empty signifiers that is overrated by a country mile. Confidence is a staple requirement in the twenty-first-century workplace; it is placed on every job advert, positioned as a must-have skill. But what does more confident actually look like, and perhaps more importantly, what does confident actually mean?[3]

Are we talking about the type of confidence that allows people at work to talk about something they haven't a clue about, or are we talking about something much more humble? I'm sure different people come to mind for different reasons when it comes to confidence – some famous people and some not so famous people. Donald Trump maybe? Did Mary Robinson, Ruth Bader Ginsberg or Jacinda Arden spring to mind? Most likely not; these women are courageous, humble, unassuming, but also confident, yet they don't shout or make poorly considered assumptions about their ability. They work hard, pay attention to detail, and they present their considered opinion with dignity and respect. Never mistaking confidence for competence but in possession of both, these women display courage and humility.

Ask: Do I have the competence to be courageous, to think big and act small, and one small step at a time move forward? Do I have the courage to try hard and to stop when I need to? Can I with humility ask for help and speak up for what I need? Or am I not sure because I'm afraid of failure and that makes me fear what others might think?

This is what is meant by dig a little deeper, to really uncover the truth beneath the data. Doing so may lead you to lamppost moments. A lamppost moment is a sudden, unexpected stop as you travel an otherwise predictable space.

I learned to read in a time before phonics, and when reading out loud in class was required. We had one teacher who used to make us read from a book, a surprise book or maybe even the newspaper, every week. There was no preparing for it and no way to know what words you would face. I used to worry the night before about what I would do if I was asked to read, and I came across a word that I couldn't pronounce. My father, not a great reader himself, advised me to read as quickly as I could, and if I came to a word that I was stuck on, I should, with pace and low tone, say 'lamppost', then raise my voice and continue to read. He advised that this might spare me the wrath of that teacher, and it did. But, he said, write the word down in your homework journal. We'll look up what it means, he added, and learn to say it when you come home. And we did that as well.

So if you come to a lamppost moment, don't ignore it, or allow it to stop you as you move forward. Pause, either now or later, learn to understand why it happened, figure out what you can learn from it, and explore the information that it presents to you.

Pause for 60

As you Pause for 60 to think about the nature and name of the challenge, be very clear about what it is. For example, is the challenge how you feel about what is involved? Has it anything to do with what others think? Are you restricted because you believe that you aren't entitled to achieve this challenge? Are there financial aspects associated with the challenge? If so, what are they? Do you feel challenged because the path to change looks scary or long?

Name your challenge and inform yourself about the nature of it. As always, this is not an exhaustive list; rather, it is one to get your creative juices flowing, to get you thinking, and to focus your attention. What processes are involved in achieving this challenge? Here you might consider the need to upskill, reskill or retrain.

As you engage with this activity and beyond, keep your focus on figuring out your data. The devil is in the detail; what you know now prepares you for what you do next, and then for each subsequent step. Only knowing part of what you need to know may be the reason something doesn't work out for you. This is particularly true when you think about financial and time commitment. Underestimating the amount of money or time that you must invest, or overestimating your ability are the most common slips that people make at this stage. For contingency, always add 10 per cent extra for time and money on top of what you need.

If you must upskill, reskill or retrain, what is the investment of time, money and resources? Is this practical and possible for you during this season of your life? Where can you go to study these courses? Is it possible to upskill, reskill or retrain online? Most of the major world players in the field of educators offer online professional qualifications from basic minimum credit modules all the way up to PhD level.

Depending on the qualification, it may even be possible to do the course through a hybrid model of live online lectures and tutorials, once-per-term in-person lectures and small group sessions. For other courses it is possible to complete full professional-level qualifications online. And for others it is in-person only. While the trend was shifting towards different forms of educational delivery, Covid-19 has pushed this forward to the point that some education institutions are only offering online engagement.

If this is something that interests you, here are some questions that you should ask:

- Is this a hybrid model or fully online delivery?
- What is the course duration?
- Is the course fully accredited by relevant professional bodies? (This may not be relevant, but professional accreditation and memberships for a course does mean that there is a standard the course must meet.)
- If something outside of my control happens and I can't continue my studies for some reason, is it possible to exit with a lesser qualification, to take a break in my studies or to complete the programme over a longer timeframe?
- If the opposite happens, can I expedite my studies?
- How much does the course cost?
- Can I pay my fees in stages or must the entire amount be paid at once?
- What modules are on the course?
- How is overall course grading weighted for exam versus continuous assessment? (If you perform better under continuous assessment than exams or vice versa, then knowing this is really important.)
- What is the time commitment?

I know what you're thinking – if it says 10 hours I could do it in seven at most, five if I tried really hard! And maybe you could, but those hours are not an estimate, they are based on the information gathered from students from previous years – so maybe you are able to speed read and put information together for assessment really quickly, and if you are I am in full envy of you, but if you are like the rest of us, 10 hours means 10 full hours, maybe even more!

Best-laid plans

In 2019 I began studying a part-time postgraduate course at the University of London. It was the first time in several years that I'd been studying in earnest and I was really excited about it. Starting this course was my challenge. Shortly after starting I became pregnant with our fourth baby, just as Covid reared its ugly head, then lockdowns followed and home-schooling hit hard. All the while I was breastfeeding and nurturing a newborn while caring for a 20-month-old and their two older siblings. As we progressed into year two, I realised that my challenge was now unsustainable. Not only had my non-negotiables been usurped, they had totally disappeared. Neither of our babies was sleeping through the night (though, thankfully, our older two children were), we were under quarantine rules and home-schooling in isolation, which meant week after week we had our children at home. My partner and I were like ships passing in the night as we tried to keep our home and respective businesses afloat.

Balancing precariously between the night shift and the early morning shift, we were both about to burn out rather than glow up. As a couple we manage better the more time we spend with each other; other couples may need less, and for some the less time they spend together the better their relationship! Knowing how we work as a couple and understanding how to cope as individuals meant that something had to give, otherwise, we both would.

I don't give up easily (my partner calls me a scrapper), so when I made the decision to pause my studies it was a damn hard one. But it was the right thing to do at the time, for me and for us. I felt really torn by the decision, and shifted between feeling like I was doing the right thing to believing it was the wrong thing to do. My harsh inner critic told me that I was giving up, and that if I just tried a little harder, I could manage.

But when I looked at the 168 hours a week that I had to spend, I saw that this was not a challenge I could sustain any longer. My partner began to shift his work around so that his travel time away was limited and he restricted the number of projects he took on. Doing this bought us time and space to breathe and to live. This was not an easy choice, but it was the right choice during that season of our lives.

My point is that just because you write down your next challenging step, or even if you start to live it and you find that it collides with this season of your life in an unsustainable manner, it does not mean that you must continue no matter what. Pressing pause is always an option; saying not now, or not yet, may be the most reasonable option for you.

This is not opting out or showing signs of weakness. Rather it is showing up for yourself with self-compassion, and that requires strength and courage, especially when things are tough.

So write, explore and engage with each of your potential next challenging steps. You don't need to be confident in your ability, but have the courage to show up for yourself and, one small word or doodle at a time, write it down.

When a hobby becomes a career

Think about the sets of skills that combine to make your future sustainable career real. What are they? What lights you up about learning those skills? What raises questions? What worries you? Dig deep here and remind yourself that there is a difference between a hobby and a job. The pleasurable things in life, the things you turn to for recreational pursuits, are often top of the list when it comes to a career. I have seen this time and again. The fitness lover becomes a personal trainer. A DIY enthusiast sets up a business as an upcycler. A foodie becomes a café shop owner.

Turning your hobby into your career comes with a health warning. Hobbies as part of your recreational life by definition help you to switch off from your paid work and pave the way for you to enter into relax, rest and unwind mode. In fact, the word 'recreation', as mentioned earlier, means to physically create again, or to make better. If your hobby becomes your career, what do you do to re-create yourself?

Of course this does not mean that making your hobby your career is the wrong choice. It means it must be considered.

Pause for 60

Pause for 60 and remind yourself that you are exploring all options at this stage, and a vital part of that is considering potential pitfalls or something that you might otherwise have overlooked.

It is important to ask yourself, if you decide to make your hobby your career, what recreational activity are you going to replace it with? Are there any risk-free ways that you might be able to explore this opportunity? This is where a side hustle can come in handy.

Side hustles

Side hustles are a tried and tested way to give something a go without giving up your full-time role. A side hustle involves keeping your full-time job while building a business based on your idea in your spare time. There are many famous success stories that speak to the value of side hustles, and they are certainly inspirational.

I know many people who built their business alongside working full-time; for some it worked, for others it was a disaster. Side hustles can see people working all hours of the day and night while never feeling fully engaged in work, in life or in their career, failing to feel a sense of depth and rigour in anything, all while reaching levels of exhaustion that may lead to burnout.

Again, this doesn't mean that focusing on a side hustle is necessarily a bad thing, but it is something to be aware of and to consider. I myself did it for a year. It involved 4 a.m. starts and midnight finishes, and it soaked up every ounce of energy I had. In fact, I feel tired thinking about it now! Would I do it again? Yes, but only if I really had to.

What would I have done differently? First I would have moved to a different job, one that I could clock in and out of and do with my eyes closed, with little or no stress. While doing that I would focus my energy on building my business. If possible, I would reduce my work hours until my business was generating enough income to pay me.

Pause for 60

As you Pause for 60 you are concentrating on the multiple possible ways to explore your challenge in a (relatively) risk-free manner. Is part-time work in the industry you want to work in an option, so that you can gain experience and insight? Could you volunteer in the sector? Do you have time on evenings or weekends to invest in this idea?

As you come to the end of thinking about your next challenging steps it is important to consider what would change for you should you decide to take this step. What would remain the same? Think about any of the empty signifiers that you wrote down and ask yourself – what do they really mean to me?

When you think about the skills and abilities that you need – what do they mean to you? You might, for example, consider yourself to be an innovative and creative problem-solver, but what does that mean to you? Is this only in some circumstances and some contexts or could you be that creative, innovative problem-solver in all circumstances?

For these are the core skills required for surgeons, project managers, game designers, lawyers, engineers, book editors, software developers, rapid responders and accountants, to name but a few. Those same skills are also three of the skills listed by the World Economic Forum as fundamental to employability in the future. So if these are your skills, or the ones you want to grow, what do they mean to you and how are you going to apply them in the next phase of your career? Do you have some of the necessary skills already? If so, what are they?

What will be the likely impact of this move on your non-negotiables? How do you feel as you explore the next chapter of your sustainable career story? What is your experience of living that life and career? What changes and what stays the same? How do you define success in this next chapter?

Take a breath before you continue.

A dream on paper

Your next activity is to dream on paper. It starts with you writing down the big dream, the idea, that thing you would do if you had no other worries or responsibilities. It is your dream, not anyone else's, so no matter what its contents are, no matter what shape it takes, now is your chance to activate your Permission Mindset and, in the fullest sense, allow yourself to dream on paper.

What would you do if you won the EuroMillions and money no longer dictated what you could or could not do? After the debts are paid, after the round-the-world holidays, after all the celebratory nights out, what would you do with this, your one wild and wonderful life? There are no limits, no practicalities to consider, only options and opportunities.

What career would you choose? What job would you do? What industry would you work in? Your dream might be anything from deep-sea diving to saving the Great Barrier Reef to working in your local shop, or anything in between. It might require money to achieve, and it might not. You may need to go back to retrain.

It doesn't matter what your dream is, it only matters that it is your dream job, role or career, one that lights you up when you think and talk about it. What job are you doing? Where are you working? Have you moved geographical location? Who are you working for or with? What role do you play in that organisation? How much money do you earn? Who is with you?

Pause for 60

Be as detailed as you like. In practice, some clients like this to take the form of a job advert or a description of the perfect job. But rather than this being written by someone else, you write it for yourself.

As you project yourself into your future dream career, ask yourself how do you define success? What does it mean to live a life while making a living? What does success mean to you from a personal and professional perspective? Does it involve getting out of the race to the top or staying in that race? What are your values, and how do you employ them in your work, job or career?

> What impact do you want to have? Are you driven by altruistic endeavours in the charity sector? Or is money your core driver? Do you want to build an idea from scratch and scale that to sell? Would you prefer to retrain to do something personally meaningful? Do you want to scale to a position of leadership or management in your role? Will you own the business or work as an employee? Would you like to have flexibility in your role? What are the important factors for you in this role? The world is your oyster.

As you design your dream version of success, remind yourself that you contain multitudes, each full of immense potential. Some of that potential will remain unexplored, while other parts of it will become the potential that you explore. Your dream job doesn't have to be something audacious. It may be an idea steeped in innovation and scalability. It might be finding a good-enough job, one that gives you time to explore everything else that you want to do in life. The dream, whatever it is, is your dream. Uncouple it (like Gwyneth Paltrow and Chris Martin) from the myths that drive careers, allow it, allow yourself to breathe it. Give it space on paper, and explore it. This is your future sustainable career.

Searching questions

To be sure, these are searching questions, and they are hard to answer – after all, you are trying to describe someone who exists only in the future and predict if you will like that person and what they do. But this is a draft, a rough copy of what is to come. It is not a sign of incompetence, or of failure, if you are confused by the data that has tumbled from your pen. The imperfect evidence that it represents is complicated, tricky and disordered, and to get it down on paper will involve *lots* of ordering and reordering, drafting and redrafting.

You may not know this, or at least it was news to me, but by the time this book finds its way to you, it will have gone through at least eight edits. For some reason I had presumed that all writers were brilliantly skilled, and that each manuscript was published with little or no intervention. Well, I was wrong! While the ideas and concepts are mine, they are based on evidence from many brilliant minds from the world of psychology, and sage advice from wise family members, friends and colleagues. The words you are reading did not fall onto these pages with grace; they were refined multiple times through the skills of the many professionals involved in the publishing process.

These words, held together in this way, are the distillation of years of hard work, listening with intent, learning at every opportunity and thinking deeply. The words on these pages are living and breathing, and each of you will interpret them uniquely, from your own perspective. This is the editing process, and it is ongoing, replete with multiple deletions of and amendments to thoughts as you remove some musings while reinstating others. It is through this process that you come to understand yourself, ultimately learning to thrive, flourish and progress in life *and* your career, through a sustainable career.

Write and rewrite. Visit and revisit. Give space to your ideas and thoughts. Allow yourself to dream on paper. Consider connections between the next practical step, challenging step and the dream. Look for themes that connect them to each other and to you. What does a hybrid of those possible future selves look like?

At all stages activate your Permission Mindset, for it is in that space of cognitive freedom that you will find the 'right' answer during this season of your life.

CHAPTER 10

Next Steps

Two roads diverged in a yellow wood,
And sorry I could not travel both
And be one traveler, long I stood
And looked down one as far as I could
To where it bent in the undergrowth;

Then took the other, as just as fair,
And having perhaps the better claim,
Because it was grassy and wanted wear ...
Robert Frost, 'The Road Not Taken'

When HarperCollins contacted me to see if I was interested in writing a book on the changing world of careers, and specifically on the growing sense of work–life imbalance felt by so many, I was in equal parts thrilled and scared. I had always wanted to write a book but never thought I would get the chance to do so, and with a publishing house of their stature behind me, well that was the cherry on the top.

That was December 2021, almost exactly a year ago to the day as I write these words. The time was right for the idea. We had just emerged from Covid-19 and the world was opening up again. We knew that something was shifting in how we thought about our careers, and the world of work. What we didn't know, nor could we predict, was the sequence of events that would unfold before us as a team. As the saying goes, you couldn't make it up.

Over the course of writing this book, as the seasons of our respective lives shifted and changed, so too did our '&s'. Of the many people working on this book, collectively we have experienced myriad momentous moments: the birth of a new baby, the passing of a family member, a serious health diagnosis, concerns over the health of family members, house builds, home moves, exams, new dogs and sick children.

Sitting alongside these momentous moments, the career shocks and catalysts, the 'normal' hustle and bustle of life continued to accompany us in the background. We went on holidays, took days off to switch bank accounts and stayed at home due to severe weather warnings. We worked half-baked days after weddings, book awards, Christmas parties and other important family celebrations.

This book was written and edited at kitchen tables, in hospital waiting rooms, in offices, at home desks, in coffee shops, hotel rooms and in the car park of football pitches. As we did so, rain, snow, frost, sunshine and a soft summer passed by each of us.

The when, where and how of this process is important because it reveals the reality that as we worked on this book, and committed whole-heartedly to it, each of us had our lives happening all around us.

To facilitate the season of life we were each living through, the team involved have never all sat in the same room face to face. Geographical distances, alongside a list of '&s' in our corresponding lives, have made doing so impossible.

But we have spoken by phone, met virtually and exchanged voice notes. At different junctures and for different reasons we panicked, laughed, talked, collaborated and communicated in a way that has brought us to publication. At times, there were tears of frustration, but we spoke to each other about them, and reminded each other that while this is important, there is a bigger picture beyond it, so moving, shifting or taking the road less travelled is not just OK, it's the right thing to do.

This could never have happened if it weren't for a focus on the person doing the job, or the human behind the title. Coupled with compassion, kindness and understanding as the need arose, we made changes. Our communication was clear, concise and candid but always kind, and shared with the warmth of the person sending it. This meant deadlines shifted, phone calls moved, and timelines were recreated so that each one of us could pour our best selves into this book. Asking for those changes or flexibility *never* suggested a lack of interest, or a decline in commitment to the book or to our careers.

Freelance, part-time, new recruits, full-time permanent and self-employed people of all ages, during a variety of seasons of life, worked side by side, and contributed with heart. Our work patterns were each distinctly different. Week-on week-off work, full-time remote work, full-time hybrid work and a reduced work week were tethered to each other, and as we found a tempo that worked for us, we relied on each other's unique skill set to bring this book to publication.

Yes, there were times that it was hard, really hard. There were some late nights, and early mornings. Personally, my husband and I had to pass like ships in the night while our four children were sick in order to stay afloat in our respective jobs. Editing this book was one of the hardest, yet most rewarding things I have ever done.

As you read these words, know that this book is not just the theory of a sustainable career, it has found its way to you by ensuring that each person involved experiences a heartfelt sense of entitlement to access a sustainable career. One in which it is possible to thrive, flourish and progress in life *and* in your career.

Our '&s' sit at the centre of our respective careers, forming part but not the entirety of our identities. Our seasons of life are different, wildly different from each others', but by looking for points of connection, and activating our Permission Mindset, the experience is one in which possibilities emerge.

So what does that mean for you and your career?

What you know

In the pages of this book, you have found facts, data and time for reflection, each one chosen to support you as you challenge the assumptions underpinning the myths of working life and the broken world of work we are living in.

Armed with this knowledge, it is possible, for you at the individual level, for groups at organisational level and for the collective at societal level, to question these deepest-held beliefs that impact how we make decisions on a personal level and how those decisions are influenced by the wider values of our cultural, social and political systems.

As you reset your relationship with your career, you begin to question why the thing (your career) that theoretically should be a source of joy and meaning is, for many of us, a great source of pain, making us sick as we attempt to live life while having a career.

As you reset your relationship with your career, so that you find a sustainable career, one in which you thrive, flourish and progress both in your life *and* work, remind yourself that though the path you have chosen is challenging at its core, all the while it can be deeply rewarding. It requires you to step into your inner hero as you break the rules that no longer serve you. Courage is your friend as you disobey the codes that previously blocked access to opportunity to anyone, and everyone, who is not WEIRD, a blockade that held so many people back from exploring the full potential in their life *and* career.

As you journeyed into a sustainable career throughout the course of this book you have in each Pause for 60 moment collated and collected the personal data required to help you design your own version of success during this season of your life. At each prompt, you activated your Permission Mindset and allowed yourself to freely go with your thoughts, as you explored alternatives to deeply held thoughts and assumptions.

Pause for 60

So, before we go any further, Pause for 60 and remind yourself that you are incredible and full of potential. If things have not worked out the way you would have liked them to, don't blame yourself; the silent rules that operate in our environments have not been kind to many of us. But armed with the knowledge that you have equipped yourself with across the pages of this book, know that it is possible to thrive, flourish and progress in life *and* in your career.

As a quick recap, you have within the pages of that notebook (the one that makes you smile) the words, doodles, mind maps and visuals that together form the evidence you need. You may now recognise whether your own career is an unsustainable one, and whether you need a fresh perspective. You hopefully now have the tools to break through patterns that no longer serve you to better understand what a sustainable career is. In one Pause for 60 after another we aimed to figure out which season of life you are living your career in, the deeply interconnected relationship between the personal and professional, and how that impacts your decision-making process.

You encountered your momentous moments, made up of the career shocks and career catalysts that got you to this moment in time. As you took a raw and unfiltered Career Selfie, you established where you are in your career *now* with a view of understanding a more personal definition of success in the future. Understanding and designing that version of success through the lens of a sustainable career means establishing your non-negotiables. These are your physical, personal and professional non-negotiables, or boundaries, that help you as you reset your relationship with your career, so that it feels OK to protect your yes and own your no, as you navigate the broken world of work.

As you do so, remember that you are not alone, that there is a tribe, *your* tribe out there, who are willing and ready to support you as you learn to thrive, flourish and progress in life *and* in your career.

Before we wrap it up, two last things: know your support circle; and find an accountability buddy.

Know your support circle

Your support circle is a Ronseal term, in that it does exactly what it says on the tin. It consists of the people who support you as you design your version of success. These are the people you turn to on a daily, weekly or monthly basis to find support, help, love and encouragement. They are the people who make you smile, shine light and love into your world and who, when needed, with kindness and candour, tell you just what you need to know, even if it's not what you want to hear!

The members of your support circle are different for each person. They may be any combination of family, friends, colleagues, help (paid or unpaid), medical professionals, counsellors, religious advisers or other professionals.

As you think about this, you will know what I mean. Who do you turn to for a cuddle? When something is wrong, and you don't have the words, who is the first person you think of? Who is the person who always steps in to sort out a problem? What about the person you go to when you need a shoulder to lean on, get parenting advice or deal with a work issue? Who do you turn to when you want the kids picked up last minute or when your pet needs to be minded? When you feel like you need some fun, who do you ask to go out? If you need motivation, who do you call?

These people might be close by, or you may be geographically separated, but you know who they are. These people are your inner support circle, the people closest to you, who are there for you and you for them no matter what.

As you shift from thinking about your inner circle, widen your lens a little more and ask, who is your next layer of support? Who do you turn to in work? Is your boss or line manager part of your support circle? If so, what role do they play? Do you have a mentor? What is their role in your support circle? What about the angels who come in the form of babysitters, childminders or early years educators and teachers? If you are a parent, each of these people is in your support circle.

Figure out who is in your support circle and for what reason. This helps you see the dotted lines between your life, your career and your work. It also highlights the deeply interdependent nature of life, and the fact that no person, not even the most efficient of us, does it alone.

As you paint the picture of who is in your support circle, share with each person how important they are to you. Explain how much gratitude you feel for the role they play in your life, and in helping you to write the story of your future sustainable career.

Find an accountability buddy

An accountability buddy is a person who works with you to keep you on track and who commits to check in with you daily or weekly. Ideally, this person is someone far enough removed from you to be objective, and who with candour offers insight when you need it, unafraid to hold you to account for what you have chosen to do and ready to show kindness at the right time.

You don't need someone who is rude or unkind – that isn't accountability, that is something else entirely. What you need is someone willing to ask the hard questions, make you face your reality and, when needed, to be kind. And you should be kind to yourself as you write the story of your support circle. You may wish that a certain person played a different role than they do, and you may feel sad that they don't live up to your hopes. Perhaps the person you most want in your support circle has passed away. Some of the people in your support circle may also be the opposite of support in some ways and your rock in other ways. No single person is likely to tick all the boxes, nor is anyone likely to be 100 per cent good at each support that you need.

Your world

Knowing who is in your world, who is there for you, and in what guise, you remind yourself that you are not alone in your endeavour. We are all together in our collective desire to reset our relationship with work, and to reassess how we live life and earn a living.

As you harness the energy and power inherent in a sustainable career, one designed by you for you, use this acronym for success:

See your goal.
Understand the obstacles.
Clear your mind of doubt.
Create a positive (but realistic) mental picture.
Embrace the challenge.
Stay on track.
Show yourself you can do it.

As you prepare for SUCCESS, stay true to your innate human power to create, and innovate – in fact encourage it to accompany you. Continue to write, draw, doodle and mind map just as you did in each Pause for 60. Find moments to read history and poetry. Embrace art and drama. Listen to music and go to gigs. At each turn, question with the relentless curiosity of a four-year-old asking 'why'. Explore widely.

By doing so you aim high in your life *and* in your career, as you design your own version of success. Follow the natural ebb and flow inherent in the seasons of your life, be true to them, and true to yourself. Reset your relationship with your career so that you can thrive, flourish and progress in your life *and* in your career, not one or the other. Capture your brilliance within this new framework, so that the future of work is a bright one for us all.

FURTHER READING

Below are a number of books which I find continually useful and enlightening, and which you may find useful resources for further reading:

- On relationships, I recommend *The Secret Lives of Adults* by fellow Irish psychologist Allison Keating (2018).
- On sleep and how important it is, check out Alex Soojung-Kim Pang, *Rest: Why You Get More Done When You Work Less* (2017).
- On data bias and the problem that it presents for everyone, see Caroline Criado-Perez, *Invisible Women: Exposing Data Bias in a World Designed for Men* (2019).
- On new ways of thinking, try Nesrine Malik, *We Need New Stories: Challenging the Toxic Myths Behind Our Age of Discontent* (2019).
- On the importance of nutrition for our well-being, read Daniel Davey's books *Eat Up: Raise your Game* (2019) and *Eat Up: The Next Level* (2022).
- On burnout, find Siobhán Murray's *The Burnout Solution: 12 Weeks to a Calmer You* (2018).
- On creativity, anything you can read, watch or listen to

by the incredible Professor Ken Robinson. Start with *Out of our Minds: The Power of Being Creative* (2015).
- On neuromythology and the myth of the gendered brain, check out Gina Rippon, *The Gendered Brain: The New Neuroscience That Shatters the Myth of the Female Brain.*

ENDNOTES

Chapter 1

1. Gallup, *State of the Global Workplace: 2022 Report* (Gallup Press: 2022)
2. American Bureau of Labour Statistics, 'Labor Force Statistics from the Current Population Survey', (U.S. Bureau of Labor Statistics: December 2022)
3. Eurostat figures on active job seekers are from the Eurostat report 'Key figures on Europe: 2022 Edition' (Flagship Publications: 2022)
4. Leclerc, Christophe, et al., 'OSH Pulse – Occupational safety and health in post-pandemic workplaces' (European Agency for Safety and Health at Work: September 2022)
5. McCord, Mark, 'Workplace well-being: Stress increasing since COVID-19 began', World Economic Forum, 12 July 2022
6. Pega, Frank, Náfrádi, Bálint, Momen, Natalie et al., 'Global, regional, and national burdens of ischemic heart disease and stroke attributable to exposure to long working hours for 194 countries, 2000–2016: A systematic analysis from the WHO/ILO Joint Estimates of the Work-related Burden of Disease and Injury', *Environment International*, Volume 154 (2021)
7. Puthillam, Arathy, 'Psychology's WEIRD problem', Monk Prayogshala Research Institution, 15 April 2020

8. Henrich, Joseph, et al. `The weirdest people in the world?' (*Behavioral and Brain Sciences* 33(2 -3), 2010)
9. Broom, Douglas, 'Home or office? Survey shows opinions about work after COVID-19', World Economic Forum, 21 July 2021

Chapter 2

1. Gould, Stephen Jay, *The Mismeasure of Man: The definitive refutation to the argument of The Bell Curve* (WW Norton & Co., 1996)
2. *Education at a Glance 2022: OECD Indicators* (Organisation for Economic Co-operation and Development: 2022)
3. Allocations Calculators 2022/2023, Institute of Guidance Counsellors, 2022
4. Spengler, Damien, et al., `Sixteen going on sixty-six: A longistudy of personality stability and change across 50 years', *Journal of Personality and Social Psychology* (American Psychological Association): January 2023
5. Hardy, Benjamin, *Personality Isn't Permanent: Break Free from Self-Limiting Beliefs and Rewrite Your Story* (Penguin: March 2020)
6. Costa, Paul, et al., `Personality across the life span' *Annual Review of Psychology*: 2019
7. Roberts, Brent and Mroczek, Daniel, `Personality trait change in adulthood', *Current Directions in Psychological Science*: 2008
8. Krivkovich, Alexis, et al., *Women in the Workplace*, 2022, McKinsey & Company, 18 October 2022
9. 'Women and Men in Ireland in 2019', Central Statistics Office, 30 April 2020
10. National Childbirth Trust, 'NCT research finds women are ending maternity leave sooner than they would like', NCT, 30 May 2014
11. Donovan, Sarah, 'Paid Family and Medical Leave in the United States', Congressional Research Service (Congressional Research Digital Collection): 13 June 2022
12. 'Parental leave systems', Organisation for Economic Co-operation and Development, December 2022
13. Jackson, Jamie, 'Cristiano Ronaldo and Georgina Rodríguez announce death of baby son', *The Guardian*, 18 April 2022

14. Cox, Josie, 'Paternity leave: the hidden barriers keeping men at work', *Worklife*, 13 July 2021
15. Press Statement: 'Employment Analysis of Maternity and Paternity Benefits 2016–2019', Central Statistics Office, 2 June 2020
16. Perry, Mark, 'New research from Denmark finds that motherhood and a 'child penalty' are responsible for the gender earnings gap', American Enterprise Institute, 23 January 2018
17. 'Modern Family Index shows motherhood penalty in American workplace', Bright Horizons, 28 January 2019
18. Drydakis, Nick, 'Sexual Orientation and Earnings. A Meta-Analysis 2012–2020', Institute of Labour Economics (IZA and Emerald Group Publishing): June 2021
19. 'Global Gender Report 2022', Abstract, World Economic Forum, 13 July 2022
20. Gender Balance in Business Survey, Central Statistics Office, 12 July 2021
21. Babic, Audrey and Hansez, Isabelle, `The glass ceiling for women managers: antecedents and consequences for work-family interface and well-being at work', *Frontiers in Psychology*, 9 March 2021
22. *How's Life? 2020: Measuring Well-being* OECD: 9 March 2020
23. Press Statement: 'Pulse Survey May -June 2021 - Life at Home: Snapshot of Results', Central Statistics Office, 22 June 2021
24. Lupu, Iona, et al., 'Role distancing and the persistence of long work hours in professional service firms', Organization Studies, 26 May 2020
25. 'Grant and Gluek Study', Adult Development Society, 2015.
26. Wilkinson, Crystal, et al. 'Exploring the work–life challenges and dilemmas faced by managers and professionals who live alone', *Work, Employment and Society*, 9 February 2017
27. Cox, Cody, et al., `The Baby Boomer bias: The negative impact of generational labels on older workers', *Journal of Applied Social Psychology*, 6 December 2017
28. 'The menopause at work: Guidance for people professionals", Chartered Institute of Personnel and Development, 9 August 2022

29. Zaval, Lisa, et al., `Fluid and crystallized intelligence', *Aging and Decision Making*, 2015
30. Trafton, Anne, 'The rise and fall of cognitive skills', *MIT News*, 6 March 2015
31. Said-Metwaly, Sameh, et al., `Does the fourth-grade slump in creativity actually exist? A meta-analysis of the development of divergent thinking in school-age children and adolescents', *Educational Psychology Review*, 19 June 2020
32. Macdonald, Kelly, et al., `Dispelling the myth: Training in education or neuroscience decreases but does not eliminate beliefs in neuromyths', *Frontiers in Psychology*, 10 August 2017

Chapter 3

1. Gladwell, Malcom, *The Tipping Point: How Little Things Can Make a Big Difference* (Little, Brown: March 2000)
2. Klotz, Anthony, 'The Great Resignation', *BC News*, Boston College, November 2021
3. 'Number of quits at all-time high in November 2021', TED: The Economics Daily (U.S. Bureau of Labor Statistics: 6 January 2022)
4. Parker, Kim and Menasce Horowitz, Juliana, 'Majority of workers who quit a job in 2021 cite low pay, no opportunities for advancement, feeling disrespected', Pew Research Center, 9 March 2022
5. Welpe, Isabell, 'Taking a closer look at the bidirectional relationship between meaningful work and strain at work: A cross-lagged model', *European Journal of Work and Organizational Psychology*, October 2021
6. Cedefop, 'Inventory of lifelong guidance systems and practices – Finland', CareersNet national records, 2020
7. Valls, Stephen and Schor, Juliet, `What do platforms do? Understanding the gig economy', *Annual Review of Sociology*, July 2020
8. 'Job tenure in turbulent times', The European Union Labour Force Survey, European Union: 2015
9. Employee Tenure Summary, Economic News Release (U.S. Bureau of Labor Statistics: September 2022)

10. O*NET in the US, run by the US Department of Labor and European Skills, Competences, Qualifications and Occupations. is found at onetonline.org.
11. Wigert, Ben, et al., 'The Wellbeing-Engagement Paradox of 2020', Gallup, 13 March 2021
12. 'Long working hours increasing deaths from heart disease and stroke: WHO, ILO', World Health Organization, 17 May 2021

Chapter 4

1. Gender and Economy, or GATE, part of the Rotman Institute of the University of Toronto, has brilliant and accessible information on all topics in this chapter. While gender is the entry point to exploring many complex issues, the research uses a lens of intersectionality to broaden perspectives. GATE can be found online at gendereconomy.org.
2. Inclusion survey: 'Uncovering Talent', Deloitte.
3. For more about the problem of work-life balance check out the academic work of Joan Acker. This article is an excellent starting point: `Hierarchies, jobs, bodies: A theory of gendered organisations', *Gender and Society*, June 1990

Chapter 5

1. Levinson, Daniel and Levinson, Judy, *The Seasons of a Woman's Life*. (Knopf: 1996)
2. To find out more about Donald Super and the career development movement this article is a really helpful place to start: 'Most Frequently Cited Career Development Theories', Career and Awareness Preparation, Pennsylvania Department of Education.
3. For more information on the autobiographical perspective see this article by Sheldon, Signy et al., `A neurocognitive perspective on the forms and functions of autobiographical memory retrieval', *Frontiers in Systems Neuroscience*, 29 January 2019
4. Seasons of liminality: meaning and understanding, information and further reading can be found at Larson, Paul, `Liminality', *Encyclopedia of Psychology and Religion* (Springer: 2014)

5. Scholarly information on liminality and identity construction is found in this article: Beech, Nic, 'Liminality and the practices of identity reconstruction', *Human Relations*, 23 September 2010
6. More information on the concepts of occupational limbo and prolonged periods of sensitivity is found in this journal article: Bamber, Matthew, et al., 'Occupational limbo, transitional liminality and permanent liminality: New conceptual distinctions', *Human Relations*, 12 June 2017
7. Dir. Williams, Tim, *After The Roar: Brian O'Driscoll explores men's mental health in retirement*, BT Sport, 21 September 2022

Chapter 6

1. To find out more about emerging research on the role of career shocks in contemporary career development check out this article: Akkermans, Jos, et al., `The role of career shocks in contemporary career development: Key challenges and ways forward", *Career Development International*, September 2021
2. For more information on momentous moments, unexpected career turbulence, shocks and catalyst start with this article: Akkermans, Jos, et al., `Tales of the unexpected: Integrating career shocks in the contemporary careers literature', *SA Journal of Industrial Psychology*, April 2018
3. Details on sexual harassment in the US can be found in the US Equal Employment Opportunity Commission 2020 report 'Sexual Harassment in Our Nation's Workplaces' (U.S. Equal Employment Opportunity Commission: April 2022)
4. If you are triggered or impacted by the content on sexual harassment in the workplace, please contact your local Rape Crisis Centre, Samaritans, or national helplines. If you are based in Ireland please contact the Dublin Rape Crisis Centre: www.drcc.ie. If you, a friend or a loved one are considering reporting sexual abuse and violence the DRCC is a safe place that provides a listening ear 24/7.
5. An article on Harvard's Happiness Study titled 'The secret to happiness? Here's some advice from the longest-running study

on happiness' is on the Harvard Health Publishing website. There is an equally brilliant and highly engaging 2015 TED talk by its lead researcher Robert Waldinger: 'What makes a good life? Lessons from the longest study on happiness', TED, 23 December 2015

Chapter 7

1. Boring-Bray, Wendy, 'Behavioural health providers are burning out or rusting out', *Psychology Today*, 21 September 2021
2. What is rustout - not burnout - caused by occupational boredom? For more information on this phenomenon see Leung, Mei-yung, et al., `Adjusting stressors - Job-demand stress in preventing rustout/burnout estimators', *Surveying and Built Environment*, June 2007
3. Statutory entitlement to paid annual leave is protected by the European Union under Article 7 of the Working Time Directive. Specific details for each member country can be found on the European Observatory of Working Life – EurWORK website.
4. The benefits of annual leave and taking your allocated time off is discussed in research published in 2022 by the Royal College of Surgeons in Ireland: 'Evidence why you should use annual leave – and how to make the most of it', Royal College of Surgeons Ireland, 18 August 2022.
5. You can find a great round-up of the latest research on UPTO and its impact in de Bloom, Jessica, et al., `Unlimited paid time off policies: Unlocking the best and unleashing the beast', *Policy and Practice Reviews*, 24 March 2022
6. University of Essex and Economic and Social Research Council, 'UK Household Longitudinal Study: Capturing life in the UK in the 21st century', is available to view at www.understanding society.ac.uk

Chapter 8

1. O'Regan, Eilish, 'Sitting is "the new smoking" for inactive employees' Independent.ie, 9 April 2016

2. For more information on decision-making fatigue, start with this blog post by Washington State University: 'Decision fatigue: What it is and how to avoid it', Carson College of Business, 2022

Chapter 9

1. More information about Cathal Gaffney can be found on the Brown Bag website. This interview with Irish Central covers his career progression: Bushnell, Niamh, 'One Irishman's journey from losing a Garda job to an Oscar nomination', Irish Central, 21 September 2016
2. The godmother of job crafting is psychologist Amy Wrzeniewski. To find out more about the nuances of it and how it might (or might not) apply to you, this article, co-authored with Jane Dutton, is really helpful: 'What job crafting looks like", *Harvard Business Review*, 12 March 2020
3. The problem with confidence and its necessity for 'all' jobs is a field of growing research. You can find out more in this article: Hack-Polay, Dieu, 'Are graduates as good as they think? A discussion of overconfidence among graduates and its impact on employability', *Education + Training* 9 July 2020

ACKNOWLEDGEMENTS

This book began with an unexpected email that found it's way into my spam folder, alongside an email from the Prince of some far flung country offering me untold wealth, in the middle of December of 2021. I had just returned to work from my fourth maternity leave and I quickly realised that the email was from Catherine Gough, of HarperCollins*Ireland*, and that it was in fact for *me*. Soon after, Catherine and I chatted virtually and I agreed to develop and subsequently to write this book.

Writing a book is something I have always wanted to do. It's a journey made up of many thousands of conversations, thoughts and experiences, contributed to by many people. It is at once a singular and shared act, something which I could not have achieved on my own. In many ways the process of writing a book is a reminder that the support of others is both a powerful source of motivation and inspiration. From those conversations and shared experiences the evolution of many ideas began.

To my parents, my mum, Mairead, and my pops, Tony, who instilled in me a love of learning and the value of working hard from the my earliest days. My big little brother Sean, big due to his height, small as he is four years my junior, is my greatest friend. Loyal and trustworthy, candid and hilarious he has been a constant in my life. His wife, Deirdre, is more than a sister in law, she is my friend, and together they form a warm, kind and formidable duo. Their three beautiful children (my nephews) Tiranán, Fionn and Caoimhín, fill our world with joy giving the best hugs, dancing to *Encanto*, and watching *Buzz* together.

Almost exactly twenty-one years ago to the minute as I write my acknowledgement to this book, I met Alan, my life partner (more about him in a moment). And when I did I found a second place to call home. His parents Eilish and Barney, welcomed me into their lives with open arms. Alongside his brothers Brian and Enda, and sisters Síobhan and Paula, they welcomed me into their home and lives with a warmth and openness that you could only wish for. The fun and friendship, alongside the love that I have found with them is beyond measure. Not to mention the addition to the ranks of my fellow 'out-laws' Paul, Ollie, Hannah and Julie. Together we have grown into a clan of many. And as we did I became a very proud aunty to Áoibhe, Ornáith, Lauren, Daithí, Charlie, Alfie, Lucy, and Cleo – who give warm hugs and jump for joy each time we meet.

My husband, Alan, is my rock and soul mate. Finding each other in Lanzarote while living just five miles from one other was a lottery win. This past twenty-one years we have navigated the world side by side, and as we did we found our place in it as partners in the deepest sense of the word. Together we have grown into parents to our four wonderful children, Saíbhe, Saórla, Siún and Senán. They are our greatest gift to each other and they are our future. Thank you to each of my babies for reminding me to take breaks, and for never failing to enjoy the simple things in life. This book is my ode to you, and your future.

I have a small group of wonderful people who I have the privilege to call friends. To the Merville Madams, Laura & Helen, my dearest friends, you are my world. To Aisling and Eileen, alongside Damian and Barry, our worlds are brighter with you in it. Carol, who, from table tennis to swimming, has been there every step of the way – thank you. To my newly formed adult friends, the ones that I have recently met, Allison, Oonagh, Daniel, Taragh, and Kathryn – you are a constant inspiration and our conversations have shaped the outcome of this book.

I am grateful for the opportunity to share this journey with the people who have supported me along the way. From my first educators in St Mary's Castlerahan, to St Oliver's in Oldcastle, you sowed the seeds of this book many moons ago. More recently, I am indebted to Professor Micheal O'Rourke and Dr Uracha Chatrakul Na Ayudhya, who challenged my thoughts and provided a critical perspective through which to view this world. To Émer, a soon to be psychology graduate, thank you for your thoughtful and insightful support during the writing and edit of this book. Your research was second to none.

I am privileged to be part of the ACORNS community led by the formidable and brilliant Paula Fitzsimons. Paula offered me the hand of support, and a community to back it up, in 2015. Since then she has firmly stood in my corner offering support and kindness whenever and wherever she, Orla and Clodagh, could possibly do so. My lead entrepreneurs Anne Reilly and Lulu O'Sullivan alongside my fellow female entrepreneurs made staying in and growing a business possible. I am forever indebted to this community of women.

It has been a great privilege to work alongside the HarperCollins*Ireland* tribe. Patricia, Courtney, Fionnuala and Ciara. My editorial team at HarperCollins*Ireland*, initially Catherine, currently on maternity leave, and now Stephen, I cannot imagine doing this without you in my corner. Stephen your dedication to this book at every turn was immense, your advice sage and your warmth felt beyond the virtual space where we met. Conor, your advice and constant source of reassurance when needed and compassion when required were keenly felt. These words are my toast to you each one of you. The words are mine but the honours are yours.